Kathy—

I hope this book,
along with my love and
friendship, will help make
your 34th year, and all the rest to
follow, very happy for you.

Love, Chris

FLYING SOLO:
The New Art of Living Single

FLYING SOLO:
The New Art of Living Single

by Kenneth Wydro

Published by
BERKLEY PUBLISHING CORPORATION
●
Distributed by
G. P. Putnam's Sons, New York

G.P. Putnam's Sons and the author wish to thank the following writers and their representatives for allowing excerpts from their works to appear in *Flying Solo:*

"YOU'VE GOT TO HIDE
YOUR LOVE AWAY"
(John Lennon & Paul McCartney)
Copyright © 1965 Northern Songs LTD.
All rights for the USA, Canada, Mexico, & the Philippines controlled by Maclen Music, Inc. c/o ATV Music Corp. Used by Permission. All rights reserved.

"SUZANNE"
(Leonard Cohen)
© 1966, Project Seven Music, Div. C.T.M.P., Inc. 120 Charles Street, N.Y.C. 10014 reprinted with permission.

"WHERE OR WHEN"
(Rogers & Hart)
Copyright © 1937 by Chappell & Co., Inc. Copyright renewed. Internat'l copyright secured. All rights reserved. Used by permission.

"The Elephant Is Slow To Mate"
From THE COMPLETE POEMS OF D.H. LAWRENCE, edited by Vivian deSola Pinto and F. Warren Roberts. Copyright © 1964, 1971 by Angelo Ravagli and C.M. Weekley, Executors of the estate of Freida Lawrence Ravagli. Reprinted by permission of The Viking Press.

"HEARTBREAK HOTEL"
(Mae Axton/Tommy Durden/Elvis Presley)
Copyright © 1956 by Tree Publishing Co., Inc. Internat'l copyright secured, all rights reserved. Used by permission of the Publisher.

"JUST LIKE A WOMAN"
(Bob Dylan)
Copyright © 1966, by Dwarf Music. Used by permission. All rights reserved.

"TEACHERS"
(words and music by Leonard Cohen)
Copyright © 1967, Stranger Music, Inc Used by permission. All rights reserved.

SBN: 399-12151-X

Library of Congress Cataloging in Publication Data

Wydro, Kenneth.
Flying solo.

1. Single people. I. Title.
HQ800.W93   301.4   77-27287

PRINTED IN THE UNITED STATES OF AMERICA

To my parents
and to the angel of light
with whom I wrestle
both day and night

I wish to thank all the participants in the "Singles Night at Hunter" class for sharing their inside stories and for their friendship. For their support, love and encouragement, special thanks to Lee Thompson, Betty Lipton, Michaele Lawton, Agneta Eckemyr, Jane Minion and George Olthof. For her good cheer and goodwill, appreciation to Betsy Nordstrom, my editor. Finally, without the spiritual food and humane vision of my teachers, David LeGrant and Rudolf Steiner, this book would never have even been started.

Contents

PROLOGUE   11

Chapter One:
TIME ON YOUR HANDS   17

Chapter Two:
THE WHEEL OF FORTUNE   35

Chapter Three:
BREAKING THE ICE   71

Chapter Four:
ROLES AND SCENES   93

Chapter Five:
THE TWENTIES: FLYING THE COOP   107

Chapter Six:
THE THIRTIES: SATURN RETURNS 127

Chapter Seven:
SEX AND LOVE–THE DEAR FORBIDDEN FRUIT 147

Chapter Eight:
TUNING YOUR INSTRUMENT 165

Chapter Nine:
I OFFER THESE SEEDS FOR YOUR FEAST 191

Chapter Ten:
THE NEXT TIME IS THE FIRST TIME 197

Prologue

By choice or by chance, more and more people are opting to live single.

Why?

What is this phenomenon, this impulse to reexamine, re-evaluate and redefine traditional psychosexual relationships? Why are people waiting years to get married or choosing divorce or simple cohabitation as an alternative to "tying the knot"?

Essentially being single provides an individual with variety and mobility. It is a time of life to enjoy, to explore and to discover more about who you are as an individual. Although there are times of doubt, fear and loneliness, being single holds many advantages in our society.

The most positive approach you can take to being single is to see it as a time *given* to you which provides you with an opportunity to develop your individuality and to create the quality of your own existence. In a paradoxical way, being single is *more* responsible than being married, engaged or paired off because you have to take care of yourself by yourself. The single person is the author of his—and her—own book, and since there are so many options and roads to travel, making decisions on *how* you want to live is both a challenge and a terrifying experience.

There is no doubt that being single confronts you with yourself, and some people do not like to look at themselves. They look in the mirror and draw a blank. Other single people are hunters, in desperate search for the ideal mate, someone else to guide, to complete and to give meaning to their lives. Still others give up all search and lock themselves in secret closets with trapdoors, preferring to seal themselves off in fantasies or recriminations, entertaining ghosts of the past and visions of what-could-have-been.

Yet there are many others who make the most out of being single, who find the life-style adventurous and exciting, demanding and rewarding. This book is aimed at those who want to enjoy their freedom and put this time to positive use. Some suggestions in this book are directed at the social single, presenting ways to meet and enjoy other people, while others are directed at the private single, offering ideas on how to meet and enjoy yourself.

If there is any golden rule for making the most out of being single, it centers on liking and enjoying yourself. There are too many reasons to feel depressed, lonely and neglected. Moreover, there are many social, family and psychological pressures surrounding both single men and single women. The purpose of this book is to change the negative to the positive and provide stimulating alternatives within the single life-style.

In this book I am speaking as a man who has always been single but who has never been out of love. Women and love have always played an essential role in my daily affairs, and for me, love will always be the bottom line. But in this book I speak for more than myself. In the fall of 1974 I was asked to lead a course at Hunter College's Center for Lifelong Learning called "Singles Night at Hunter." This noncredit, experimental course drew men and women from all ages, backgrounds and professions, and much of the material in this book is a result of listening to their stories, situations and dreams.

Over and over again these singles reported to me that they enjoyed being single the most when they were *not* looking for a partner. Situations seemed to develop and opportunities began to arise when they were simply being themselves and being involved in activities that they enjoyed doing. When they were absorbed in and enthusiastic about an activity, others seemed to find them. The most important directive in making the most out of being single, then, is to determine specifically what you want and to make a commitment to yourself.

With that objective in mind, I offer this book to help you lead a fulfilling life as a single person, no matter what your age, sex or romantic track record.

If you should write out answers to the questions suggested in various chapters, by the time you finish reading this book, you will have written one of your own. That is what flying solo is about—getting ready, learning to wait actively, and contacting the creative spheres.

FLYING SOLO:

The New Art of Living Single

CHAPTER ONE

Time on Your Hands

Being happy being single is no accident. Those who flourish under the condition seem to have developed and nourished a certain attitude about themselves and their time.

Their secret is to convert wasted, tentative time to positive, committed time. Since many singles have time on their hands during evenings, weekends and vacations, it is possible for them to turn nonproductive time into a time of growth. No matter what your business or social schedule is like, taking time every day to review the day and to look at yourself quietly and calmly provides you with a space to grow, to change and to find alternative ways to get what you want.

One of the most successful human beings I know, who also happens to be single, is a young man-on-the-go from Willmar, Minnesota, who is an active lawyer in New York City.

"My greatest luxury and my greatest source of inspiration," says J. R., "is my hot bath every night. No matter what else happens during the day, I make time for that hot bath. I find that those fifteen minutes of relaxation and solitude give me fuel to continue and provide me with a better sense of myself. I play back my day in pictures, as if I were watching somebody else, and I plan out my day tomorrow. I try to think of where I want to be and what it will take to get there. That bath is my sanctuary. If I skip it, something seems to be wrong with my entire day."

J. R.'s hot bath is a positive act which has reverberations on many levels. First of all, it provides him with a period of relaxation and retreat from the hectic, demanding business of the day. On a strictly muscular level, hot water soothes and cleanses, while his action of reviewing his day and watching himself as if he were another person builds an *objectivity* in and *distance* to his own actions. The solitude of his own bathroom becomes a private screening room where he can get a view of himself and his actions that in turn provides him with a sense of where he is and where he is going.

The hot bath time has become a habit for J. R., one which he consciously makes happen for himself. He sees this time as crucial to a positive sense of himself.

"Taking my hot bath every day sometimes takes a great act of will. There are always many unexpected things that come up during the day, but when I neglect that bath, I experience a certain negative attitude change in myself. That one act of will, taking my hot bath and reviewing my day, has become my turning point. Taking that time for myself every day gives my life a purpose and a shape, and I now find it essential to my frame of mind and emotional outlook."

J. R. put his finger on a power principle when he characterized his hot bath as an act of will. Many single people who are unhappy and anxious display a similar trait—the paralysis *of will.* They start and stop. They find reasons for not doing things. They are tentative about what they want and how to get it. They prefer to blame family, society or economic conditions for their isolation and loneliness. But most of the time the source of their unhappiness lies within themselves and in their inability to carry out an act of pure will.

J. R.'s bathtub does not get filled by itself. There are many days when it is easier or more convenient to skip that time. The bath has become for J. R. a symbol of his will. Every day that he slips into that bathtub for his fifteen minutes of relaxation and self-reflection, he strengthens his will and his ability to carry out an intention.

He *makes time* for himself, which is then reflected in his attitude about himself. He is not outstanding in his talents or in his personal appearance. What makes him different from most people is that he feels good about himself. He knows he can set a goal and execute it.

Jasmine L., a manager in a personnel office of a major Wall Street brokerage firm, is less cerebral and more sensual about her acts of will, framing them in romantic and sensuous colors.

"I dance in front of a full-length mirror for ten or fifteen minutes a day—more if I have time. I put on some music and work out the tensions of the day with a limbering-up routine. I took some dance classes in college and like to dance to popular current styles. I keep in shape and keep up with the times by doing this every night.

"When I miss a night or two, I just go back. I don't kick myself or get down. I just dance. In my own house, where I can be as crazy as I want or as graceful as I want. But that time is for me. I *need* that time for me!"

If you do anything with focus, purpose and concentration for fifteen minutes a day, you will be proficient within a very short period of time. This daily routine of taking or making time for yourself can lead to genuine self-confidence. Taking time every day for a hot bath or a dance routine often triggers ideas, feelings and intuitions which will allow personal style and grace to flourish.

"A short time after I made dancing a routine," Jasmine continued, "a great idea came to me. Once a week I gave myself the task of taking as much time as I could with one activity. Since I felt so good dancing regularly, I decided to spend a whole afternoon shopping and preparing dinner with a new friend of mine. I met him at a party, and I proposed that we have dinner together at my place starting at one P.M. on Saturday afternoon. We went out food shopping, took a walk in the park and eventually cooked dinner together, and by doing those things together in a casual, relaxed way, we really got to know each other.

"The whole idea of taking as much time as we could appealed to both of us, and all during the day we talked about what we were *doing*. We talked about the importance of taking time and sharing. It was nice and easy. Cozy."

One of the first realizations that comes from the quiet time is that being single allows you to do what you want. You have the freedom to determine the quality of your own life. You have yourself as the center.

"But isn't that selfish?" you might object. "What good is life if you have nobody to share it with and you think only of yourself?"

But what is it that you have to share? What is inside you that is *able* to give, touch and love? What is positive about yourself that someone else would want?

Some singles have physical beauty, and others mental agility. Some have financial resources, and others brash confidence. Many have doubts and fears that something is wrong with them because they are single. Some are plagued with a gnawing anxiety that they are undesirable and cut off from the good life because they have not found partners.

For many single people the most important task is keeping a positive frame of mind in periods of loneliness, isolation and doubt. The *idea* of being single is sometimes the most aggravating element of being single, so the quest to find your *center* becomes something to do to fill the empty space.

Being single allows you the time to explore your individuality and to come to terms with your own sense of yourself and who you are. At some point many single people of both sexes take an existential turn and ask themselves some of the more elusive and challenging questions of life:

Who am I?
What am I doing here?
What is the purpose of my life?
Is there a reason why I am living, and is there a reason why I am living single?
How much of this is my own creation, and what can I *do* about it?

Strange as it may seem, this line of questioning and self-examination starts in a person's mid-twenties and surfaces with full impact in his or her twenty-eighth or twenty-ninth year. Two chapters of this book will be devoted to the inner psychic and social changes that many people experience at twenty-one and twenty-eight years of age. There is a definite inward turn about age twenty-eight. There is a questioning of the self and a desire to come to terms with an unconscious past and with a set of potentials which have not yet been realized.

This inward turn takes a great deal of courage and a willingness to accept the idea that every individual creates his own reality. At the deepest psychic level everyone is the author of his own book. It is always difficult and painful to gain an inside track on yourself. Being single requires that an individual first make peace with himself.

It begins to dawn on many single people that no one else is to blame for their condition but themselves. Consciously or unconsciously they have chosen their own destiny, and if they feel bad, unfulfilled or despondent, they themselves must initiate a change.

Centering is a method of initiating change and coming out of a shell of loneliness. A good way to start is to take time for yourself in a daily, regular way. Making time expressly for yourself, in a hot bath or a quiet bedroom, will often bring you into contact with deeper psychic levels of your being. These are the levels that need to be dealt with by any person, of either sex, in order to find a center.

The centering process *can* lead to a certain fear, anxiety and existential anguish, but many people report just the opposite effect. Taking the time to be quiet, to read, reflect and plan ahead leads to a more positive attitude, especially when an individual wants to define and accentuate the positive elements of his being. When you, as a single person, practice the art of self-centering, in the sense of consciously determining needs and directions from within, you also learn how, what and when to give. Determining your own internal program leads to a confidence and an ability to act. Confidence, courage and commitment can be built up through a self-determined and self-actualized activity like taking a hot bath every day.

The key factors in centering are *everyday self-determined* and *self-actualized* actions. They should depend on you alone for completion. They come from within you and are activated by you without anyone else playing a part. There will always be good reasons to skip the bath or fall asleep without taking time for yourself. There will be phone calls to make or people to see. Duties will demand attention, and friends will want time. But what about yourself? Consciously doing something for yourself every day has a magical effect that cannot be conceived of from an intellectual point of view.

Self-centeredness does not mean that everything in the world has to center on you. Self-centeredness means that you have an inner center, a core and a focus out of which you operate and to which you can refer back for guidance.

Martha S., a handsome thirty-seven-year-old divorcée with an eight-year-old daughter, discussed one of the most plaguing problems that a married woman with a child has in terms of a lack of a center.

"My marriage broke up because I was no longer happy in

my role as wife and mother. All my actions were centered on my husband and his affairs. It started from the very beginning, on the first night of our honeymoon, when he asked me to wash out his socks. His mother used to, he reasoned, so why shouldn't I?

"Then he wanted a monkey in the house. He thought it would be fun. A monkey. Yes, a real live monkey that used to swing on the walls and leave dirt all over the place. My husband laughed and went out to work, and I was left to clean up the mess. I played my part, but the role I programmed for myself was that of *I have to be taken care of.* The man acts and the woman reacts, and I bought that script until I didn't like myself anymore."

Martha's divorce was lengthy and bitter; the alimony battle, bloody and emotional. But it was something that had to be done for her peace of mind and her sense of herself.

"There are money problems and court appearances now," she says, "but at least I feel I am my own person. That's worth the hassle for me."

So much of living single depends on how an individual *sees* himself and his time. The quality of being your own person— of having time, making time and using time for yourself—is the most positive trait you can develop. Many women like Martha learned to define themselves in societal roles, and only later in life do they realize that there is more to them as individuals than what society and family say they are "supposed" to be.

Martha felt guilty about her own needs and desires, and when she began taking time for herself by writing in a journal, a new dimension began opening up for her.

"Writing in my journal was a burden at first, something else that came from outside that I had to live up to. But after that initial period of *making* myself sit down for fifteen minutes a night, I soon looked forward to that time when I could put on paper what *I* felt and what *I* wanted. I saw qualities in myself that I had never seen before when I read over what I had

written a month or two later. Writing every day helped me
gain an inside track on myself. Since I was doing it for myself
and by myself, I also felt a great sense of accomplishment.
After only six months *I wrote a whole book!* Not that I want
to publish it or anything, but writing a whole book is really
something."

Martha was beaming when she talked about her book, and
with a little encouragement, she shared some passages that
seemed funny, sad or significant to her. She was taking the
time to do something creative, something that did not cost
money and did not demand time away from her home or her
daughter.

The fifteen-minute period before bed was Martha's time for
herself. She used it to talk to herself about the day just past
and the day to come. By writing about the events, the people
and the unexpected happenings of her day, she began to see
some patterns more clearly. Soon conclusions and concepts
she had taken for granted were questioned and examined in a
different light.

"For a long time I believed that my thoughts and my
feelings didn't count for much. After I began writing for
myself, the words on the paper gave my inner life a weight
and a validity that were not there before. Once upon a time
what I wanted and felt were vague sensations, but the act of
writing them down made them more real, more accessible,
more workable.

"Writing in my book gave me a sense that I counted, that I
meant something as an individual, and whether I was married
or not didn't mean that much. One day the idea came to me
to give my book to my daughter when she was old enough.
On her sixteenth or eighteenth birthday perhaps. A book
written by her mother in her mother's own handwriting, just
so she could see where I was coming from and what I had
been through. The idea excited me for weeks, and now, when
I write, I write not only for myself but with the idea that
Suzanne will sit alone on some rainy night years from now
with the inside story of her mother's life. Whew!"

* * *

Whether it is writing, learning a foreign language or playing a musical instrument, a creative outlet you can practice in your own home can be an essential building block in making the most out of being single. Single people do have time for themselves. Many find that starting a creative activity gives a shape and a dimension to their lives and opens doors that they had never thought of before. It doesn't matter whether you think you are creative now. Some people think that they have nothing to write and no creative talent, and that is simply not true. There is a creative pocket inside all of us, and the effort to find it often uncovers some glittering suprises.

There is one very subtle and powerful exercise which always works for people who are willing to stick it out to the end. It is an exercise which brings to light taken-for-granted skills while it expands your consciousness of yourself. The exercise is simply to *change your handwriting* consciously. If you write in script, start to print. If you print, start to write in script. If you do both, start to stylize your writing by doing calligraphy. Set aside fifteen minutes a day to look consciously at a skill which you perform unconsciously. Buy a blank book and work intensely for a few minutes a day. When you finish look back, and see what you have carved out for yourself by an intention to change. The difference in self-concept from beginning to end shocks many people because it brings them a certain confidence that they can execute a goal of self-development and self-expansion.

Some people have found that taking a book that is a classic, one they have not read since high school or college, and copying the book in longhand, word for word, leads to some fascinating and rewarding results. By slowing down and taking time with an activity, by performing that activity consistently and consciously, they become aware of hidden talents. By the time they have finished a book with depth and substance, a book by Goethe, Faulkner or Dostoevsky, for example, something is stirring inside themselves that was dormant.

One woman of a more mystical, religious and spiritual

nature chose to write out the Gospel of St. John. When she became sick and bedridden for a period of time, the idea came to her to memorize the whole Gospel. Years later she reported that the accomplishment was the major achievement of her life, something that stayed with her and gave her a constant source of inspiration. The quality of her entire existence changed for the better from that moment on, mainly because she had performed an act born out of herself, by herself and for herself. She subsequently found she was able to give more of herself because she had something definite to give.

Giving yourself something to do every day leads to insight into your own internal process, as well as a commitment to yourself. This kind of exercise results in an ability to finish something, a talent a good number of single people report is difficult for them. Whether it is a course or a book, a plan or a relationship, there is often a halting, tentative quality to their actions. Tentativeness leads them to look in the wrong place for answers to dilemmas. They seek magic formulas to help them, whether the task is overcoming shyness or breaking a shell of withdrawal.

A commitment to a daily effort brings to light a startling and reassuring sensation about that old devil time. In short, there is a right time to move out into the world, and there is a right time to move into the self for reflection and examination. To establish an alternating rhythm between action and reflection, between advance and retreat helps gain an inside track on yourself. Taking time to do something purposely and consciously each day for yourself builds a capacity to distinguish the essential from the nonessential.

Some singles testify that time is their greatest source of anxiety. They have either too much or too little of it. If they are not married, engaged or otherwise paired off by the time they are in their late twenties or thirties, they feel that time has passed them by or they have wasted their lives. Time is something to dread because chances for happiness and intimate relationships diminish as days and years slip by.

Time is something that happens to them because they do not use it for themselves. They tend to be spectators and critics of other people's activities. The state of being single then becomes very lonely, depressing and self-defeating.

But individuality is not a spectator sport. *Being* is an active state, a process of change and growth. In order to make the most out of being single, an individual must first be comfortable with his own time and his own space. One of the most effective ways to use it for yourself is to create a special place where you feel comfortable with yourself and others.

Kathleen G., a former college teacher and now a management trainee with a major airline, spends a great deal of her time decorating and shaping her own space.

"I fill my time by filling my space. I just bought a cooperative apartment for about the same money I was paying monthly for rent. Having something of my own was important to me. Now all my leisure time is centered on making my space my own. I like the idea of having my living quarters reflect my individuality and my personality, and I keep an eye out for things that jump out at me.

"I like to travel, and I have a job at the airline. When I am away, I always look for objects that would look good in my space. I like to think in terms of *time* and *space*. Every object in my house *means* something to me. Therefore, I see time in my space."

Kathleen is an attractive thirty-year-old divorcée who keeps herself busy on purpose. She goes to evening classes, on antique shopping weekends to Vermont and on carefully planned vacations to foreign countries. She finds making plans very important in the positive quality of her single life.

"I don't sit around and wait for things to happen to me. I place myself in situations where something is likely to happen. I always meet somebody in classes, either to go for coffee or a ride home or even to go out with on a dinner date. Each semester—being an ex-schoolteacher, I still tend to think in terms of semesters—I plan a course of study and try to fill three or four nights a week with some activity. I give myself a routine, but a routine that is always challenging me and that puts me in new places."

Taking, planning and using time for yourself helps you determine what you want. But since a surprising number of single people have not clearly defined for themselves what they want, the first step in leading a fulfilling single life is to answer some rock-bottom questions. The following exercises will help you answer these questions. They work better if you *write* your answers on paper rather than simply answer them in your head. Space is provided here to jot down some ideas if you choose.

1. What did I want *today?*

2. What did I do to get what I wanted today?

3. How did other people see me today?

4. How did I see myself today?

5. What did I do to improve myself or understand myself better today?

6. What influenced or determined my behavior from without today?

7. What influenced or determined my behavior from within today?

8. Did I set an intention or an objective to accomplish today?

9. Did I complete my intention or objective? If not, what got in the way?

10. What was the core action of the day, the event on which everything else centered?

11. Did I choose the action, or did the action choose me?

12. How do I feel about myself today?

13. What is it about myself that I like and other people seem to admire?

14. What is it about myself that I do not like and feel could be improved upon?

15. Where do I see myself a year from today?

16. Where do I see myself five years from today?

17. Where do I see myself ten years from today?

18. What do I really want, short term and long term? What am I doing every day to get it?

19. Did I take time for myself today to plan and then review my day? If not, what got in the way?

These are not easy questions, and demand more than superficial answers. Perhaps you have thought of them and have reflected on them because of your own psychological makeup. But have you asked questions like these of yourself on a regular basis—for instance, every day for a month?

Some people in the Hunter singles class experimented with these questions for a thirty-day period, writing down the answers to the same questions on a daily, conscious basis. They reported that doing the exercise every day led them to a greater commitment to themselves. They became more conscious of their actions day by day. They began to fashion more directed behavior out of their own inner lives. They developed more positive attitudes about themselves.

They also reported that taking the time to answer the questions for a month was a devilishly difficult task. Life circumstances seemed to conspire to get in the way, or they didn't feel like answering the questions, or they were too tired. The commitment to an objective of self-evaluation, even for a short period, like a month, was elusive.

Many found themselves to be "swinging singles"—not the glamorous, carefree, high-living type, but the ones who swing from the idea of liking the freedom and mobility of being single to the idea that it is essential to share a life with someone else. While looking at themselves in a regular way, they discovered how deep their couple orientation ran. Some of them felt a sense of being wrong or inadequate because of being single. Others found that they thought being single was only a temporary condition and that at some stage of the game there would be a mate or some kind of intimate relationship.

For many, what emerged from these questions was a sense of being *in between,* not really being happy with themselves and not really wanting to be with someone else. There was a manic swing back and forth from wanting and needing to be alone to wanting and needing to be with another person. This ambivalence colored every action, making them tentative and unsure, which led to withdrawal, which led to self-re-crimination.

One conclusion was certain: There are no magic formulas to make the most out of being single.

Just the idea of taking time for yourself and sticking to a plan of action is a positive start. Taking the time to develop yourself contains a principle of love. When you set out on a course of self-examination and self-determination, you often discover that being single is primarily *a time of preparation.* As a single person locates and develops a center of confidence within himself and defines what he wants, he becomes more able to give of himself and to enter a relationship. This relationship may be with another person, a group or a creative hobby. Whatever the form, there is a sense of giving yourself to something outside yourself and thereby realizing yourself.

One of the most positive aspects of being single is that the individual has many relationships, interests and sources of stimulation. Once there is an inner confidence and a willingness to explore the parts of yourself that are now hidden, situations develop almost by themselves. The hardest work is within the self. It is the coming to terms with the self that is the most intriguing aspect of being single, as we will discuss in the next chapter.

Make an effort to review your day as if you were looking at

another person, distinguishing the essential from the nonessential. Successful single life has most to do with the efforts you make. If you make these efforts with consistency and enthusiasm, results will fall into place.

That's where the Wheel of Fortune comes in.

CHAPTER TWO

The Wheel of Fortune

For many people, being single is a dead-end street. Without a partner or a current love affair many are lost souls, hanging onto threadbare fantasies of how love should be. Romances have fizzled out time and time again. Engagements have been broken at the last minute. Marriages have lost meaning and purpose. It often becomes easier to sit home alone and seal themselves off than to put themselves out on the limb of love again.

Some fantasize marriage as a panacea—a magic, instant cure—all for isolation, depression and loneliness. These singles want marriage so much that it becomes the impossible dream, impossible because energy is invested in the wrong place. They look for the answer from an outside source when, in reality, the key lies within.

Unless these singles take themselves in hand, they will get fewer chances to find that idealized mate or any mate at all when time puts on a few pounds around the middle and a few wrinkles on the brow. As men and women grow older—a fact that lies outside anybody's control—they tend to become more rigid and cautious. They often experience a leveling off and a repetition of frustrating emotional patterns. Many learn to live within limited horizons and shut off any expectations of love because they are not *married.*

"There was a time when I thought I could get married whenever I wanted to. Someday there would be that special woman, and it would be a natural course of events to tie the knot," an attractive man in his mid-thirties confessed. He works as a director in the sales training department of a large corporation.

"I was always involved with a woman on a sexual, romantic level, and I thought getting married was just a matter of time. All I had to do was wait and be patient. Providence would take care of the rest. I didn't believe the old wives' tales about a bachelor's becoming so set in his ways that he loses his capacities for love and cohabitation. I didn't believe those stories—until I felt it happening to myself.

"I had evolved my own rhythms, my own interests and my own ways of doing things exclusive of all other people. I didn't plan it that way, but since I lived most intimately with myself, I pleased myself first. I then found myself indifferent to most situations which demanded that I give something. I was flying in my own orbit, an orbit which rarely, if ever, connected with any one else's.

"I championed my freedom and individuality but then I began to feel that I could not—did not want to—live solely for myself. I felt comfortable with myself but had to reach out beyond myself for meaning. It would have been so easy to pull the covers over my head and find fault with everyone else. Instead, I started to make conscious commitments to other people, places and causes. Only then did I begin to feel a forward movement."

In this one man's experience lies the great dilemma of being single. There is a need to get *into* and *out of* the self at the same time. Too much focus on yourself while establishing your own ways can isolate you from people. Too much focus on your need for other people to complete your life can drown you in fear, doubt and anxiety. There arises a dual need, a balancing of energies and a recognition that change is the *normal* pattern of action.

How can you get into and out of yourself at the same time? How is it possible to put yourself through some changes which will place you closer to your destiny?

This is where the Wheel of Fortune comes in.

Imagine yourself as a wheel with six spokes and with six sections constituting the total wheel. Each segment represents a different element in your total well-being. All six segments have to be in proper alignment for the wheel to roll smoothly. If one segment is out of proportion, the wheel will be like a flat tire, limping and bumping along the highway.

The six elements to be balanced out are:

1. The personal self—your relationship with yourself.
2. The physical self—your relationship with your body.
3. The spiritual self—your relationship with God or higher, invisible forms of energy.
4. The social self—your relationship with your family, friends and loved ones.
5. The communal self—your relationship with your community and environment.
6. The financial self—your relationship with money and things.

The fascinating feature of the Wheel of Fortune is that *you* supply the *energy,* the *will* and the *conscious input of ideas.* When you make an effort to fill each segment and to balance the wheel, certain situations and circumstances will come to you, appearing to be fated and destined. When you are ready, you will attain what you are destined to attain, but when you are ready is up to you and what you do.

The concept that it is up to you is the most difficult one for many singles to buy because it takes a certain reeducation of themselves. In a way, you have to unlearn everything that you were taught and learn to rely on your deepest creative potentials. Living single demands that an individual take stock and invest in himself *totally*. The best investment you can make is to align your own Wheel of Fortune—seek to *balance* your inner and outer lives.

Balancing is more an inner phenomenon than an outer one. Family, friends and social circumstances will present different, often contradictory messages. As long as you are a reactor to external, circumstantial influences, you will be in a defensive posture, one that repels love, warmth and intimate exchanges. Once the inner life is developed and tuned to a point of balance, once you locate and refine your center, you can become an actor, a creator and the prime determinant of the quality of your own life. Paradoxically, being centered and self-reliant attracts quality people and opportunities; learning to fly solo is a prerequisite for the more advanced states of loving, giving and creating children. When you work consciously and systematically on yourself, understanding the need for a center, you are actually preparing for the involvement which will add greater dimensions to your life.

A young dancer-actress, born and reared in a conservative, conventional household in Queens, was having difficulties in resolving the inner/outer conflict. She had been taught to depend on a man for fulfillment, to save money for insurance against old age and to define her well-being by material objects and possessions. Only the best was good enough for her. Material comforts and secure living were the goals of her life.

Her mother began taking her to ballet class when she was eight years old. Her teacher, a professional dancer and teacher for twenty years, constantly asked her to find her center. Intuitively she knew that this center was inside, a point within from which anything could be done. The center, like the mystical third eye of the human being, was invisible and elusive, unable to be defined in empirical terms, yet was very real and omnipresent to one who learned to locate it.

For years there was a dualistic input in her psychic system. On the one hand, things and comforts were important. On the other, all actions, combinations and situations depended on her invisible center. She experienced a psychic tug of war, a duel between a consumer and an artistic mentality. The outside taught her to think in terms of material objects, of finding a man to take care of her, yet the inside spoke an entirely different language. The inside constantly maintained that *she* was the determining factor in her own destiny and life plan.

The conflict came to a head when she became involved with a famous photographer, a man who could produce dazzling commercial images but who could not keep his financial, emotional or spiritual accounts in balance. As an artist he commanded fees of thousands of dollars a day. His style of shooting commercials revolutionized an entire industry. As a man he could not reconcile his need for freedom and his responsibility to a wife and children.

The photographer gave her nothing material except a case of VD and an abortion. Yet he appealed to her sense of the aesthetic, to levels and planes that her family and friends could hardly imagine, much less make real in an image. She and the photographer had a psychic bonding which defied understanding on any practical, material plane. They would sit back to back in bed, in total darkness, not saying a word, but holding conversations for hours. After a couple of years of coming and going he told her that when she had first walked into his studio for a shooting, he had said to himself, "Oh, there you are. Where have you been?"

There was an instant chemistry that was attractive and destructive at the same time. Seeing only the negative side, her family and friends urged her to go to a psychiatrist, who told her she was a "very sick girl," unrealistic, unmotivated, wasteful of talent, a source of pain and concern to those who

loved her most. The doctor prescribed large doses of tran-
quilizers and other pills to set her internal chemistry straight
and to level her off in the hope of having her choose, once
and for all, to leave the photographer.

After that first and only visit to the shrink the young
woman, who reminded many people of a young Elizabeth
Taylor, pulled on her leotards and put on some music in her
apartment to work out her tensions and to "contact my
center." She was upset at the doctor, upset at her family, upset
at another boyfriend who hounded her to leave the photographer.

After fifteen minutes of loosening up and stretching, she
suddenly stood in relevé, high on her toes, then shot one leg
out and back, holding it motionless four feet in the air. She
spread out her arms like an angel and maintained the position
for two minutes while holding a conversation with a close
friend. She didn't quiver; she didn't waver; she didn't lose
concentration for a second. Then she said, casually and easily,
"If I'm so sick and unbalanced, let's see that doctor do this."

This kind of balancing act can be done only by someone
who has tremendously disciplined inner resources. By holding
the pose for so long, in such perfect form and with such ease,
the young woman was defying everyone who claimed to know
what was best for her. She was confused, torn between
conventional ideas of security and her own intuitive, artistic
psyche, and she seemed to be saying by that one act of
balancing, "I can reconcile my inner and outer life whenever I
choose. I have capacities I have not yet ever touched. When I
know what I want, I can do anything. I can concentrate my
ideas into a form that is physical and spiritual, aesthetic and
practical, ideal and real at the same time. The problem is
focus—I don't know whether to believe my mother or to trust
in myself."

Focus, balance, trust in the self—those are the inner dynamics at stake in the lives of most singles.

Whom to trust? What to want? Where to look for fulfillment? Do you shoot for the ideal, or do you content yourself with the real? Is *any*body better than *no*body? Do you attach yourself for the sake of being attached, or do you hold out for that one special involvement that you sense is waiting for you?

Generating the creative energy to make the ideal a reality is a major stumbling block for most single people. As they become older and more discriminating, they become frightened that they will live alone, without committed love, forever. For many, the ideal self has been watered down by the "realistic" demands of school, family and society. Often there is nothing ideal to shoot for because our social models are quantitative rather than qualitative.

Yet the most exciting and demanding feature about being single is the possibility of fashioning an ideal-yet-real lifestyle. Before the duties of family and parenthood demand a focusing and crystallization of time and energy, it is possible for a single person to explore the scope of his own individuality and relate intimately to others at the same time.

The Wheel of Fortune suggests a way to bring about a conscious balance in your life which will open you up to a sense of destiny, meaning and purpose in your individual affairs. The feeling of "something waiting around the corner" can then be made specific and tangible. Instead of taking the form of an idealized mate or the right man, it will take the form of a refinement of your own character. Instead of waiting for another person to complete your life and give you meaning, you can begin to be the author of your own book.

If you spin your own Wheel of Fortune, you will begin to extend yourself into the realm of the *unknown,* the *unexpected* and the ideal. Extending yourself will cause you to take risks and expose yourself to your vulnerabilities. On the other hand, the sense of a piece missing from your life will diminish. The sense that some crucial act in your drama is still in the future will fade into purposeful and directed behavior in the present.

What, then, are some of the specific ways in which these

elements of the Wheel of Fortune can be activated? What are the efforts to be made? How can the elements be coordinated into a unified whole?

The Personal Self

The element of the wheel called the personal self is your relationship with yourself and how you *feel* about your past, present and future. It is the voice within that sends you a message at the oddest moments. The voice within resides in a quiet place in the soul, on the borderline between the intellect and intuition. It is always there for consultation, but relatively few of us call on its wisdom and guidance.

The voice within is abstract and unreachable only for those who neglect to summon it, and it responds well to an invitation to be heard. To hear it, we must *learn how to listen* to subtle tones and qualities in our inner plane. To use it effectively makes a basic demand of honesty with ourselves.

The following are several techniques for establishing a contact with the voice within and suggestions for using it in a practical, realistic way.

Read Aloud

The exercise of reading aloud consists of carefully choosing a book, perhaps one you read a long time ago which has somehow stayed with you for years or perhaps one on a subject which has intrigued you but has never quite come alive for you. Then read aloud for fifteen minutes a day until you have finished the book.

An additional element to this exercise is to read aloud into a tape recorder. Many people, especially those who do not like to write, report that buying a $35 cassette recorder has been one of the best investments they ever made. Once you read aloud on tape and listen to yourself, you have a definite record of the quality of your inner color.

If you read aloud and then listen to yourself, hearing

yourself as others hear you, you will become aware of your personal quality and color. The more conscious this *personal self* becomes, the easier it is to be yourself under social conditions. As you come to define your own inner individual color, the less you have to adjust to the demands of others and the less you have to play games to please other people.

Everyone who has practiced this exercise finds that the voice within becomes more tangible and accessible. Activating the will and making the effort to see yourself objectively lead to an inner confidence and a trust in your own feelings and intuitions. People who read aloud do not second guess themselves very much, and because they have exercised their will, they are not at the mercy of social approval.

Reading aloud activates an inner system which sends out subtle signals when you are going off course. Much more work and experimentation are needed in this area of the internal tracking system, but the best story I know to illustrate this device comes from ancient Greece and Socrates.

Socrates was an initiate, with developed psychic and spiritual powers to see beyond the physical plane. Every time he was faced with a social or philosophical problem he retired in quiet to consult his daemon—his voice within, his higher self, his spiritual protector. The terminology varies, but the concept remains constant.

Out of his meditative time, when he sought to still his conscious thought, he would receive a signal. If it were proper to act affirmatively, he would hear nothing. If it were proper to act negatively or do nothing at all, he would hear a slight buzz or ringing. The signal system never failed him. He had an inner voice which he trusted implicitly.

When he was convicted, his friends urged him to take flight and leave Athens for safer grounds where he could continue to teach and study. Yet he retired to his quiet room and asked his daemon if he should stay and accept the sentence of the court. When he heard nothing, when the response to his question was silence, he asked for the goblet of poison hemlock.

The voice within had never failed him before, and now, at the moment of his death, the silence indicated that he should accept his sentence. His faith and trust in that inner guiding light were the key to all actions. It led him to wisdom because it tuned him into principles of behavior which were eternal and infallible.

Perhaps we do not have the developed internal resources of a Socrates, but the direction is clear and important. Communication with the inner higher self can lead to firm, decisive, principled actions. Contacting and listening to the voice within, sometimes called the sixth sense, can be reason enough to live. Each individual person is at work on his or her own evolution. The inner callings of the heart often penetrate into deeper regions than the head. Reading aloud can develop these inner capacities and give direction and meaning from within.

The four major objectives in reading aloud are:

1. Making sense of the words intellectually.
2. Making sense of the words emotionally.
3. Putting yourself, your colors, your rhythms into the words.
4. Listening to yourself.

Make the words come alive by what you put into them. Have fun; experiment; take some chances. Then listen to yourself. Hear when you are just going through the motions. This exercise leads to confidence and courage in social situations. Reading aloud and listening to yourself help you slow down and penetrate to a deeper level. By reading aloud only fifteen minutes a day, the reader begins to live with the characters of the book, forming "relationships" with them and if the exercise is completed to the end, the book becomes ingested into the psychic bloodstream of the reader.

The exercise then becomes a prototype for other social relationships. It becomes more natural to take time, to investigate the inner character of another person, to allow a relationship to develop at its own rhythm rather than to rush it through.

If the reader makes the effort to make the material *come alive,* he exercises his emotional and intellectual systems. Reading aloud illuminates the inner self by activating the will, the emotions and the mind. Such stimulation pays great dividends in the outside everyday life. Some definite power is built up which comes into play at moments of risk, challenge and love.

Keep a Personal Inventory Journal

As suggested in Chapter One, keeping a journal always gives more weight and significance to feelings, thoughts and actions. The act of writing down problems, conflicts, desires and goals develops a power to perceive the self and act with decisiveness. Many single people testify to the problem of repeated patterns—of falling into relationships with people who are "not good" for them, even though the first attraction is immediate and chemical.

Both men and women report that they have made the same mistake again and again when it has come to emotional, sexual investments, as if there were some self-destructive mechanism deep within which they could not contact consciously. Making the same mistake over and over, choosing a person who cannot or will not give you what you want, falling for someone who is physically attractive and spiritually bankrupt are all different shades of the same color. Keeping a journal is an intriguing, creative way to see those colors in perspective and leads to more conscious actions when repeated pattern situations happen again.

To keep a personal inventory journal, buy a blank book, one that is bound so the pages cannot be torn out. (Most large stationery stores, those which carry office and art supplies, stock these blank books.) Then every night tell a story of your day. Tell a story about someone else, but that someone else is *you.* Look back over the actions of your day. Try to see yourself as other people see you. Imagine yourself an invisible being floating at the ceiling or standing behind a one-way mirror looking into a room where you yourself are. Try to see yourself from a higher, more independent perspective.

As if you were an objective reporter, make a running narrative about the people, places and situations you encounter, making the effort to make these elements come alive again. Pay careful attention to time, place and situation to see if you can discern any principle at stake in your actions and behavior.

Then, after a week or a month, read over what you have written and look for repeated patterns.

How much of what you do is conscious and purposeful? How much is unconscious and reactionary? Do your actions and conscious choices serve your deepest desires and potentials? What issues do you have to resolve? What is the next plane or stage of action you are about to approach?

When you review your personal material, your task is to make the unconscious conscious, without casting guilt or blame on anyone, including yourself. You, as the writer of your own story, should make no judgments but should simply tell the story honestly and directly. This exercise not only builds *objectivity* but also refines *perception.* People report that they "see" more by reviewing each day and writing down the actions. Besides, they have a dynamic self-history at hand. When they look back, days from years before come rushing back with great intensity. The past is active in the present, and the personal inventory journal often becomes a prized possession.

The journal is *not* a diary, which simply lists events of the day. There are specific techniques which stimulate the recording and the perception of repeated patterns. Instead of simply jotting down feelings, try answering the following two questions every time. Over the years at the Hunter class, these questions have led to astonishing and practical insights into the unconscious life of many single people.

The first question is:

1. What did this day bring to me, both externally in events, people and situations and internally in feelings, thoughts and dreams?

When the question has been answered in writing, directly and specifically for the day, a second question to answer is:

2. What part did I play in the quality of my day?

These questions are a beginning of a personal inventory journal. They are not the only possible questions, and after a period of time, you may want to develop questions and techniques of your own. The important effort, however, is to record your inner and outer lives in writing.

The act of writing makes a difference. It provides an outlet for bottled-up feelings and brings a great sense of accomplishment. Even when reviewing the journal is painful, it is always illuminating. There often comes a dramatic change in self-concept when one writes a whole book without even trying. The act of making the time to converse with yourself is another way to build confidence, courage and creativity out of a commitment first to yourself.

Determine What You Want

Specifically.

If you are not sure, or if your wants seem to change from day to day and week to week, try first to determine what pleases you.

For example, write down ten things you like to do, ten actions which turn you on. Ten. No more, no less. If you have to think to get ten, fine. Take your time, even if it takes a couple of days. Thinking specifically about what you want or what pleases you won't hurt.

When you have listed ten actions, write down the last time you did each of these. Record the date, time and place.

In a third column, ask yourself whether you would have had included each action on a list you might have made up ten years ago. How have you changed in your appetites in ten years?

In a fourth column, indicate whether each act is done alone or with other people. If you usually do it alone, mark an A. If you do it with others, add a P, for people. If you sometimes do it alone and other times do it with people, mark both A and P. Interpret what you see for yourself.

In a fifth column, ask yourself how much money each act costs. Which acts are prohibitive financially, and which acts are special because they cost some money? Try to put both actions, some which need no money spent and some which cost money, on your agenda for the coming week.

In a sixth column, ask yourself how much time each of these actions take? How many could be done *daily* by you depending on no other person?

On a separate piece of paper or on a page of your journal, ask yourself a very basic question: "If I had $5,000,000 dollars and one year to live, what would I do?" Let your imagination run, and then add some deep thought to your initial impulse. If you had one year to live, what would you want to accomplish and leave behind as a legacy?

When you have answered these questions, preferably in your journal, study what is in front of you. What do you see about your current actions and values? What can you do about what you see? Are there any patterns you wish to keep, modify or change?

HOW TO USE THIS INVENTORY

One of life's most difficult processes is discovering what you really want as an individual. Wants sometimes shift with the winds. Like the ever-changing sea, desires are pulled by unseen currents, shaped by hidden needs, moved by mysterious forces. Very often, when someone gets what he wants, he doesn't want it anymore.

But more often that not a person doesn't want any specific thing. Sure, we all could use more money, a vacation home, a fine wardrobe. But unless some goals are defined and kept in mind, chances are that wants, desires and needs become too difficult to change.

When the answers to these questions are written down and studied, this particular inventory can help you distinguish between the essential and the nonessential. It can help you zero in on what you want consciously and what you want unconsciously. It can stimulate some thinking about yourself that will focus in on an action. It's a way of using time for yourself consciously to choose events to happen rather than have them "just happen" to you.

When you look at this list and contemplate your own answers and repeated patterns, what does it seem that you really want?

What is the connection between your unconscious undercurrents and your conscious actions? Are they working with or against each other?

Are you committed to a specific goal?

Are you committed to yourself?

Are you committed to anything?

Lack of commitment is one of the distinguishing factors of people who are single and don't want to be. Making the most out of being single demands *first* a conscious commitment to yourself through specific actions. It is not enough to think positively; the thought needs to find an *action* for the self-concept to change from negative to the positive.

Commitment to the self with an action for a period of time—thirty straight days—awakens light and love in the heart. When the personal self is taken seriously and worked with as if it were a material, tangible entity, many surprises are in store.

A finely tuned personal self always draws new people, new places and new situations. Once you prove to yourself that you can act out a simple idea, you have the power to face the unknown with the courage and confidence to take a risk in the proper situation.

Exercises like this sharpen your eye, and there is nothing more seductive than psychological perception. A person who can see into the invisible as well as into the tangible, the one who perceives the intentions as well as the actions, is always more intriguing than someone who is visceral and literal. Someone who is in touch with the emotion and idea level of reality always has a life, a color and a purpose to his actions.

Be an original—not a carbon copy. This is the challenge: to find, accept and develop what you are as an individual.

Perform a Control-of-Thought Exercise Every Day

This is one of the best ways to add energy to your Wheel of Fortune and develop your personal self.

The control-of-thought exercise consists of picking a simple object—a bauble, a spoon, a paper clip, a comb—and concentrating your thought on that object for five minutes, letting no other thoughts or concerns come into your field of concentration.

Pick up any object in front of you, and look at it carefully. Examine the form as if you were to be given $10 for every detail you see. Then ask yourself, "What is the concept behind the form?"

What *idea* preceded this object?

How did this object come into being?

What conditions were necessary for this to go from the abstract idea level to the material, physical level?

Ask yourself questions like these. Don't leave an object until you've figured it out and exhausted it. It may take one five-minute exercise, or it may take ten days of five minutes a day, but dig as deeply as you can in your effort to see the concept behind the form.

Choose a Model

Choose someone in history, someone in sports, someone in your personal life whom you admire and revere. Choose a person who you think is special and outstanding, one who is gracious, warm, understanding, someone whom you like to be with or would have liked to have known. Choose someone with whom you can make an inner connection, and *study* that person. Get pictures of that person Read his or her biography.

Determine what this person did to develop the special qualities which attract you. Become an expert on a person whom you admire and revere, actually *revere*. Too often we lose our potential for reverence and devotion. We tend to lose faith that there is an ideal to be reached. When we lose faith, life becomes flat and stale.

Keep a model in mind when you are making a decision or planning a course of action. How would this person have acted in similar circumstances? Why? What principles were at stake?

Spend some regular time studying your models. If you can, take a class on the subjects you have chosen, a class in art, or politics, or psychology—whatever and whoever interests you. Have someone who has worked in the field give you information from an expert's point of view.

One of my most stirring models is Picasso. Over my desk I have a cutout black-and-white photograph of Picasso sitting in an empty studio, clad only in Bermuda shorts and sandals, sitting on a wooden box, smoking a cigarette. The whole studio is dark, except for two pools of light—one on Picasso himself and the other on a wall where two pictures are hanging. Nothing else is present, and all Picasso is doing is looking. Staring. Watching those forms, with no distractions.

Looking, studying, looking for the depth level. The soul, the spirit level. He's working by looking.

I sometimes look at this picture when I am irritated, when I am confused and distracted by trivial concerns, when I spend energy thinking about when that right woman is going to come along. Whenever I contemplate this particular picture of Picasso, I always get a lift.

Developing a positive relationship with your personal self is more than becoming your own best friend. It involves a shifting of emotional gears and a transformation of ideas. Instead of depending on someone else to take care of your business, you begin to accept and enjoy the fact that you are your own guide, judge and master.

As you learn to take time and invest in your own peace of mind, you will become confident and quiet. You'll have a glow around you—an aura of being yourself which often attracts others *without your trying*. Working with this personal self on an everyday basis makes all social, family and professional situations *better, easier, more enjoyable*.

It's like putting your own personal house in order. Cleaning up and clearing out the ideas that don't serve any purpose. Ideas like you should be married or it's bad to be alone. Maybe it's not bad to be alone. Maybe it can be good and even necessary. Maybe being alone and loving it are the key to everything else.

The Physical Self

You are a woman in your late twenties or early thirties. You have a sound education, professional experience and a couple of romances behind you. You are intelligent, talented, sensitive, assertive, yet vulnerable. Especially about being alone, living alone, sleeping alone.

You feel that you need another spoke in your wheel for it to go around smoothly. You are looking for someone who can speak your language and travel on your wavelength—psychologically, intellectually, emotionally. You have found yourself going up the ladder in your job but around in circles in your relationship with lovers.

You have taken a new position around Thanksgiving time. Now comes the office Christmas party. You don't know anybody. There are both married and single men around and available. What do you do? How do you feel? What do you look for? What strikes your eye *first?* What are others looking at?

The first turn of the head will come about because of how you look. Most men will be attracted not by your refined inner personal self but by your material outer physical self, and there's something you can do about that.

How you look does count—but not the way many women would think. Your hair, your face, color of your eyes, your height are not as important as they are made out to be. It's the composition that is more important and more striking to a man.

A woman does not have to be a physical beauty to be attractive; it's the condition of her body and the coordination of her elements that turns heads and gives signals that the inner personal self is whole and together.

Style is more significant than physical beauty. Doing the most with what you have is the secret to an appealing physical self. It is a process of conditioning, of discovering some ideas and putting them into action in a daily way.

Two major concerns for many single women and men in the physical realm are the need for *relaxation* and the need for *exercise.* The pressure of the outside business world is becoming more intense all the time. If you are still single, you probably find you spend a great deal of time and energy in your work situation which can be as empty and aggravating as it can be frustrating. Tension is constant, and after a while tension becomes the norm. Routine becomes boring. Both conditions point to a great need to *relax.*

One of the best ways to start to condition your physical self is to take the time every day to relax, to stretch out the muscles, to release the tension of the day. Many single people carry the tension of the day, as well as the anxiety of past concepts, into new emotional, social relationships. Tension piles up very easily, and if there is no conscious release, it colors and condemns almost every new relationship.

At that Christmas party wouldn't you be attracted to someone who is relaxed and whose body is in good condition?

There are three very accessible ways to condition, to stretch and to relax the body and the psyche at the same time.

Hatha Yoga

Hatha Yoga is a special activity which has positive effects on many levels. Hatha Yoga is the yoga of the physical body, and practicing it for fifteen minutes a day has cumulative effects on the physical, psychological and spiritual systems of the human being.

The key elements of Hatha Yoga are the alternating actions of *stretching* and *relaxing*. As you can learn from the many yoga centers all around the country or from illustrated how-to books, Hatha Yoga requires fifteen minutes of quiet time every day to loosen muscles and release both physical and psychic tension.

The exercises or postures lead to a supple, flexible body, as well as to an undeniable sense of peace of mind and a feeling of well-being. As with most physical/psychic disciplines, Hatha Yoga is best practiced every day at a certain time in a clean, private, quiet place which should be seen as a sanctuary.

Once you discover where your personal tension accumulates—often in the shoulders, neck and back—there are specific postures to stretch and release the tension in those areas. Postures such as the shoulder stand or the salutation to the sun have a direct and positive effect on your entire body. It's best to start slowly with Hatha Yoga and take a few elementary classes. After a while you will be able to perform postures on your own, at home, on vacation; some people even close the door to their office for a few head rolls when the going gets tough.

Hatha Yoga is available, inexpensive and far-reaching. It is one of the best ways to get in touch with your body and change the pace of the day. It asks you to slow down, pay attention to inner processes and listen to your higher self at the same time. It always opens doors to physical and psychic health and can be the best of friends in difficult, lonely times.

Jogging, Walking, Biking

One of the most up-to-date leisure activities is jogging, and for good reason. An activity that both men and women can do together, it has direct and immediate effects on the condition of the physical body and on the sense of oneself.

In many cities and university towns, jogging is becoming a social as well as a physical function, and there is nothing more exhilarating or healthy than a mile or two jog—five or six miles are easy when you get into it.

There are several ideas to keep in mind when you jog in order to keep the spirit high and the legs pumping. Most important, you should start slowly, running only a few minutes a day for the first few times. Run as far as you can, then walk, and then run again, aiming for your fifteen minutes.

As you jog, look out around you at the scenery. Keep your consciousness focused on outside events, not on inside events. Try not to let your mind wander away, but keep it focused on the physical field around you.

As you look out, you give your psychic system a rest. Try not to talk to yourself about your day or your problems; take a break, and keep in mind what you are doing. Your task is to stretch and work out physical tension, break a sweat, *feel* your body.

Stretch your legs out before and after you run. Loosen up.

Invest in good shoes—quality is essential. Take the hills fast, and keep your focus out.

Although the emphasis of jogging is completely different from Hatha Yoga's, both provide a meditation period of sorts. Both activities (and walking and biking are included in this category) lead to definite insights into yourself as an individual. Very often characteristics you take for granted and things about yourself you do not like or want to hide come into a more positive perspective.

Again, the everydayness of jogging is important. Every day for fifteen minutes is much better than an hour once a week. You will build up strength, stamina and endurance—not to mention new, active, on-the-go friends. Jogging knows no race, sex or age barriers. It's coming into its own because it brings people together while making individuals closer to themselves as people. It is physical, psychological, emotional and spiritual. It feeds all systems and works for everybody who tries.

It beats the meat market of the singles bar—that's for sure.

Dance Class

Have you ever taken a good, fast, up-tempo dance class?

No, not Arthur Murray, Fred Astaire or the Latin hustle, but a professional modern, jazz or ballet class?

Many singles never consider such an activity because they "don't know how to dance" or don't want to "feel foolish." Yet sixty or ninety minutes a week in a jazz class can change one's entire physical picture and psychological frame of mind.

There's something wonderful and exciting about moving in rhythm, swaying to music, using your body in ways you have seen only on television or at a live Broadway show. The lines, curves and moves of a dancer, either male or female, constantly remind you of the aesthetic of the human body which responds to training and effort in a very short time.

People meet people when they are sharing activities, and

dance is another one of those physical, social, emotional and spiritual actions which have reverberations on many levels. Almost everyone feels awkward and out of place in the first class or two, but if you stick it out, dance will give you a good feeling about yourself and your body.

There are more and more "professional" dance classes springing up around the country, and if you can locate a good teacher, you can be dancing, even flying, after a few months. You will walk down the street differently, aware of the dynamics of your body, head lighter, eyes wider, your feet a little above the pavement. Good dance classes make you think while you move, excercising the mental as well as the physical system.

There's nothing like the moment you "get" a combination, a series of movements put together. Once you move from your head to your heart and "feel" the music, a whole new world of improvisation opens up. Many people feel "unlocked," released, extended by a dance class which will certainly not hurt their social life either.

Dance is an excellent way to invest time and money in yourself. It helps you overcome shyness and self consciousness and gives you something to do that is positive, physical and mental at the same time.

In a secret corner of the heart everyone is a ballerina. "Have the courage of your fantasies," a famous acting teacher once said to his students. Make your reality a theater, and every moment will be filled.

The physical self can be transformed, conditioned and streamlined by ideas. If you agree that how you look is important to how you feel, then you have an idea that can be made to work for you. The condition of your body is more important than natural beauty or artificial cosmetics. The key concepts are *to relax, to stretch* and *to extend.* As you give yourself to such activities, you will soon find psychic counterparts to your physical action.

Looking good, feeling confident, being ready to take a

chance all are a matter of effort and commitment to yourself. Hatha Yoga, jogging and dancing are activities which can be done alone or in a group and which can lead to other people of the same kind.

Time must be invested. There is no shortcut to a conditioned body. But there are ways to enjoy the discipline and make your body respond to your will. A firm, trim, supple body always draws more than looks; it commands respect, and that is where good relationships begin.

If you don't know where to start making the most out of being single, start with your body. Make it your best friend by treating it with love. You will get a fantastic return on your investment—guaranteed.

The final frosting on the cake is grooming. Details count in the whole picture—clothes that fit to your body, hair that is trimmed and styled, shoes that are shined and kept in shape. Wrapping the package is often as important as what is inside.

Conditioning and grooming—each takes time and effort. But both are essential in that positive self-image which keeps your Wheel of Fortune rolling on a progressive path!

The Spiritual Self

Just as it pays to keep the physical self conditioned and in tune, it pays to keep the spiritual self alive, alert and active. The spiritual self is the element most often neglected, ignored or even denied by individuals in our materialistic society, yet the spiritual self can provide the most nourishment to sustain the individual through dark periods of doubt and despair.

The problem is that the spiritual self cannot be measured and recorded because it is composed of invisible, intangible, indefinable threads which have to be *sensed* by a mechanism that goes beyond the bounds of the five physical senses. The spiritual self is that part of the human being that is intuitive, imaginative and inspired. It is the element that links the physical, material plane to the forces that shape and guide human behavior unconsciously.

Many single people report a sense of fragmentation, of being out of touch with a plane of reality which they can sense but cannot "prove" in any scientific way. Because most of us have been taught to focus in on the here and now, we have missed the invisible actions that occur in and around us on a daily basis.

The spiritual self points to a plane which is above and beyond the physical but which has direct and powerful effects on everything we do. Great scientists such as Einstein assure us that there is a reality which we cannot sense with our normal physical tools. There are forces which can be tapped by a refined set of capacities. Our educational system, for the most part, does not train people to think clearly or to entertain philosophical principles that are difficult to grasp. Yet thinking can provide a link to these invisible planes, once the mind is trained and developed to "see" the invisible currents around us.

Developing the spiritual self is a matter of plugging into higher circuits than the ones normally used in business, sports or entertainment. The faculties of intuition, imagination and inspiration can be trained and extended so that they do not operate randomly or sporadically. Most people have experienced déjà vu, the feeling that something that is happening for the first time has happened before. Many people have traveled to a foreign country where they have never been and felt a sense of being at home or somehow recognizing the landscape. Many experience a moment of destiny when, without doing anything, events just seem to fall into place.

More and more single people are believing that there is "something higher" at stake in each and every human life. The spiritual self beckons the individual to make contact with these invisible, yet real planes of existence. The attempt to make contact, to plug into higher circuits often provides a lifelong course of interest and study, one which gives a reason to living and offers social exchanges at the same time.

There are some definite, specific ways to establish contact

with the spiritual self within you, but it takes an open mind, one that is ready and able to let go of rigid concepts about what is real and what is not. As with all creative, occult and mystical subjects, there are many pitfalls and dangers, many charlatans and false visionaries. Yet there are subjects of study which open up the intuition, the imagination and the inspiration to daily conscious use.

The spiritual self is a depth psychology which can lift a person out of the doldrums into the plane of reason, evolution and mystery. For many people, there is an inner reason why they were born. Finding that reason, uncovering their psychic and physical pasts lead to committed, purposeful and fearless futures.

Modern philosophers proclaim that the spiritual self is a great void. When an enlightened person speaks of light in a dark tunnel, he is not speaking metaphorically. Work on the spiritual self does provide a definite *light*, a path to follow, a place to go that is within all of us.

As with the personal self and the physical self, there needs to be an investment in time and energy when one works with the spiritual self. Returns are not immediate or obvious. They are more subtle and intangible, but study and experimentation often provide a foundation from which all other activities radiate. The spiritual self houses the mysterious *center;* finding the center is the ultimate task.

Here are some ways of exercising the spiritual self:

Jigsaw Puzzles

During the week between Christmas and New Year's, I found myself wide awake at 4 and 5 A.M. for five straight nights. It was not a case of acute insomnia. I was simply high on the energy of the new year, visualizing different scenes that I wished to happen.

In the past I had discovered that the process of forming mental images of specific times, places and situations could create a psychic current which, under the proper conditions and backed by genuine desire, could bring things into existence in the material plane and in a tangible form. But the process was dramatically illustrated for me by the many hours I spent during that holiday period sitting before a 551-piece jigsaw puzzle by M. C. Escher, the Dutch engraver who created works that had fish crawling off of pages and ducks flying into one another—animals springing to life from flat surfaces.

It was my first puzzle *ever,* and I learned more about my own mental and perceptual patterns in those days than I can *ever* remember. The whole process of "seeing" was opened up to me with a startling and striking immediacy, and the key to "seeing" is *visualization.*

Only when you know what you are looking for does a piece jump out of the massive jumble and into a tableau. When it does, there is always a rush of joy and a sense of tremendous victory.

There were many times when I lost faith, preferring to believe that the much-sought-for piece was lost and that the whole puzzle was one huge put on from the start. Then, at a strange and unexpected moment, while I contemplated the chaos of unrelated pieces, one of them would suddenly come to life before my eyes. I would pick it up tenderly, cradling it, and lay it to rest in its proper and predestined place.

Each piece was complete in itself, but adrift and meaningless until it was fitted in with a neighbor in a strangely intimate intercourse. Only when it rested side by side with a mate did its existence have purpose and make sense. Each piece had several "lovers," ones that touched it most, but the sense of that one piece's belonging to an entire whole overrode and overpowered its own individual existence. Each piece was important—agonizingly so when it was the only one missing out of a single block. But its place in the scheme of things became of even greater significance as the puzzle came closer and closer to completion.

As more and more pieces fell into place, I began to see the absolute, primary, archetypal importance of the *subconscious* in the process of creativity. I always found five or six pieces, pieces which I had searched for *desperately* the night before, in two or three minutes after waking. I found it best to work in short, concentrated periods, but it was also true that spending longer periods studying the original helped me spot an individual piece. No matter what the schedule, I had to spend time in a regular way, but I picked out an individual piece most often in an intuitive flash.

Each moment of discovery was delicious and exquisite and made all the efforts worthwhile. Even while working on the first one, I looked forward to starting the second by Escher, this one in color, called "Another World." My eye began to see form, color and pattern as it had never seen them before. I almost jumped for joy with the work, the discoveries, the sense of process toward completion, very much like the metamorphosis toward maturity and death, the final transformation into the other world.

The greatest moment of all came when I realized that I had been looking at the puzzle only from an *overview*.

What if I were one of the pieces, I thought, dumped suddenly onto a flat surface with the internal command to arrange myself with 550 other pieces?

What if there were some whispering in my ear that all the confusion had an order and a unity and it was my task to find the others which fitted into and around me? What if we all formed one complete picture when each of us had completed our own individual task?

Even from the overview outlook it was difficult for me to find the proper pieces, but what about seeing the puzzle from an underview—from the point of view of each piece? If I doubted at the time that all the pieces were there, what would a piece itself think if it did not have the overview consciousness working for it?

But there *was* an overview, and there was an order. Each of the pieces existed on a mental, intelligent level before it fell into place, and so it was, it seemed to me, with human beings. We both have a significance as individuals and a place in a larger picture. There is an oversoul or overview which exists to guide us and fire us with energy *if* we make the effort to contact it. Plugging into that higher circuit is what the spiritual self is all about. It exists whether we believe in it or not. It is our choice to use it or ignore it, so why not use it, enlist it, open ourselves to it for the purpose of making the self whole?

Doing a jigsaw puzzle is a great way to get to know somebody. If you don't know what to do some night on a date, start a puzzle. I'll guarantee a fascinating time.

Meditation—The Study of a Nonphysical Science

Although there has been much talk and literature about meditation, it is still an esoteric practice for a majority of people in our culture. Unfortunately meditation is loosely associated with a swami from an exotic Far Eastern land which has little, if anything, to do with day-to-day Western consciousness.

Yet meditation can be a very effective tool in coping with stress, despair and a sense of meaninglessness. It can provide any person with a key to previously locked inner resources, and when practiced with joy and perseverance, meditation can be the foundation for all other psychic structures.

Meditation is not a cure-all for all conditions and situations, but it does counteract a widespread single malady: loneliness and isolation. While it will not automatically provide a body or a companion to share, it can provide an inner strength and a will to keep trying. Practiced for a few concentrated minutes a day, meditation takes some of the pressure off the daily routine, and some forms of meditation even make one's dreams more accessible, tangible and usable.

Meditation has many different forms and techniques, ranging from Transcendental Meditation to Thought Concentration to Deep Relaxation. What all forms of meditation have in common is the change of flow of energy. Usually we look out and receive impressions from the external environment. Meditation points to an inner landscape, one which is often in a state of disarray until the gardener—you—makes an effort to cultivate that soil.

Many single people have been intrigued and have made close new friends through a study of a mystical or nonphysical science such as astrology, Jungian psychology, numerology, the tarot, the cabala, theosophy or anthroposophy. All these metasciences have roots in age-old traditions and provide challenging means to trace psychic as well as physical roots. All these systems point to a plane of reality hidden from the physical senses but active as forces in everyday life.

A deeper exposure to the zodiacal signs, the planetary energies and the circumstantial houses of the natal horoscope reveal a definite connection between the cosmic forces and the earth-plane human being. A progressive psychiatrist friend who studies astrology as a hobby swears that a natal horoscope gives as much information as, or even *more* information than, a long, involved, expensive series of psychological profiles. Like an X ray of the physical body, the horoscope must be interpreted by someone who has studied and practiced, but most people who do study come to "believe" that there is a reason for one's individuality and that there is a cosmic past and future to everyone's existence.

For many, the natal horoscope is a means of self-awareness and self-knowledge. It often awakens you to a feeling of destiny. Daily life is thrown into a different perspective through the study of astrology—and not the kind of generalized mush you read in newspapers or popular magazines. There is much more to the subject than that, and if you have any inkling about the nonphysical planes of reality, astrology provides a set of symbols and a subtle language which penetrates to the deep levels of the psyche.

The Work of Rudolf Steiner

Did you ever feel that there was "something more" available that you couldn't define or explain? Ever feel there was a part of yourself that was locked up and hidden in some psychic closet? Ever sense a force in your field that was talking to you, but whose language you did not understand?

If so, you might find the turning point of your psycho-spiritual development in the work of Rudolf Steiner, an initiate in the tradition of the Mysteries, who was also an author, lecturer, sculptor, poet, dramatist, scientist, expert on Goethe, teacher and founder of the school of Spiritual Science called anthroposophy

When I was twenty-eight, I stumbled, not quite by chance, on the work of Steiner, and I read the entire *Knowledge of Higher Worlds and Its Attainment* in one night. I found the concepts so challenging, so vast, so real that I bought twelve more Steiner books the next morning. The introduction to Steiner, a philosopher completely unknown to me in all my academic studies, provided me with a reality to the spiritual world that changed my entire way of "seeing."

Kant, Nietzsche, Freud—most of the great philosophers who have had such profound impact on modern thinking—all were dwarfed by Steiner's knowledge and understanding of the relationship between the visible and the invisible planes of reality. Steiner made sense of the great religions of the world and opened up the wider perspective on the evolution of the human soul. Although Steiner wrote in German and his texts lose some of the poetry and power in translation, his book *The Knowledge of Higher Worlds and Its Attainment* has become a bedside book for many people who feel the need for spiritual food. It provides exercises and insights into the physical world which lead to spiritual awakening. It is possible to find more of yourself through his exercises, which are finding a wide, receptive audience, especially among doctors, artists and educated people. Saul Bellow recently paid tribute to Steiner, incorporating the principles of anthroposophy into his novel *Humboldt's Gift.*

Rudolf Steiner's basic books are *Theosophy, The Philosophy of Freedom* (also known as *The Philosophy of Spiritual Activity), Occult Science—An Outline* and *Life Between Death and Rebirth.*

All of Steiner's works are difficult, challenging and rewarding reading. Working through any of these books will expand your ideas about what is and is not real in the universe. The very act of reading will cause some flurries in your inner life, possibly awakening a new sense of positivity and receptivity in everything you do. It is well worth the effort.

The Social Self

The social self is concerned with your relationships to family, friends and lovers, those people in your life with whom you have an emotional relationship. You can develop the social self by making an effort to *make these people feel special.* It asks you to reach out and give of yourself. The key is to *make yourself available*—to find reasons *to do* things, rather than reasons *not to do* things.

Start by making a list of the ten most important people in your life—people who have touched you most directly and intimately. If you are not in contact with those people, establish some kind of correspondence on a continual basis. Arrange to meet them. Plan a trip or a vacation. Open up to those people and make an effort to discover the inner ties that connect you.

One of the most special ways to build a relationship consciously is to *write letters.* Phone calls are not bad, but they get to be expensive, and they are transitory. A letter is something you can live with, get your teeth into and read between the lines. It takes a little more of yourself to write a letter, but a little more goes a long way.

Developing the social self is a matter of attitude. It asks you to seek and find the positive in other people and to give of yourself. A quality of generosity needs to be nourished and practiced, and without conscious input, sometimes this quality can rot and get stale. If you make the effort to reach out, a certain strength and confidence will begin to grow. You will find people seeking you out because of your ability to give and to make them feel special. Don't expect a lot in return. Let them surprise you.

If you don't know where to start, begin with your family. Play the prodigal son. Assume that it was nobody's choice but your own that you were born into your family, and try now to fit those pieces together.

When somebody is valuable, precious and open to you, go out of your way to let him know it. Make the world special for someone else.

The Communal Self

The communal self is different from the social self in that it points to a wider segment of society than your immediate emotional ties. It is an association with a cause or social group, an association with a certain kind of people with whom you like to spend time doing something that is socially oriented.

It can be an artistic group, a theater group or a singing club. It can be a church or business organization.

The idea is to share an activity with other people, and there are many people in America and in Europe who are feeling the urge to build a community as a refuge from the alienating tendencies of our modern world. Joining any communal group builds the sense that we all are in this together.

What group you join obviously depends on your interest and talents, but the important point is to take one or two nights a week to go out of your house and into the world around you in a nonbusiness way.

I once knew a woman from my singles class who did not like to go to movies alone. She put an advertisement in a local paper, announcing the formation of a movie club. She had a fantastic response, and she took it upon herself to be the coordinator of the group. She called a local restaurant and made arrangements to set a few tables aside. She made herself available, and the whole project turned out to be a rousing success. She invited some local filmmakers to talk to the group and got a behind-the-scenes look at how films are made. The effort came back to her with satisfaction, warmth and the sense that she was doing something for other people because she wanted to.

Start your own movie group, theater group, consciousness-raising group or whatever. Get people together, and something is bound to happen.

Give your efforts weight and meaning without trying to predict the outcome. Again, make the attempt and let the results fall where they may.

The Financial Self

Last, but certainly not least, is the financial self, sometimes the biggest bugaboo of all for singles. What we go through for money is sometimes a crime. We are asked to spend so much time, energy and effort to *make money* that we tend to forget the other elements in our constitution.

A major complaint of many singles is that they spend so much time on a job they hate, just to make a living. Their work is temporary, but it takes a great deal out of them just to make a few dollars.

Frequently single people have a difficult time keeping their heads above water because they pay higher taxes and maintain apartments by themselves.

Sometimes a financial burden limits the space and freedom single people have. Sometimes the financial aspect becomes so exaggerated that the other elements of life are forgotten. There is a common feeling that getting the financial self together will put the rest of the elements in place, but I have found that the opposite is true more often than not.

Getting your total self together is a *means* of making money. When you know who you are, *and* develop your talent, *and* act on what you want, the financial self falls into place. When people do what they want to do, money comes. You might approach a personal, physical, spiritual, social or communal group and find work in those parameters. If you are going to be a secretary, you may as well be one for the United Nations or the Red Cross, for example.

Try to combine your money-making activity with another element in the Wheel of Fortune. If you are going to be a receptionist or a salesman, why not get a job at a health spa where you can work on your own body? The idea is not to divorce yourself from your work, but to coordinate yourself with your work.

Determine what your talents are, and make an effort to find employment in a field which can utilize those talents. Don't allow the notion of financial security to dictate your actions. Even if you have to live humbly or with someone you don't like just to pay the rent at first, don't let your talent dry up because you have to pay for food, rent and clothes.

Your work should have some element of turning you on and making you grow. If you are not growing in your job, get out while the getting is good and you are still young.

If you do clerical work, seek a job at an airline, for example, something that has benefits for your social or leisure time. How can your job work for you outside your office? Make it a definite goal to get that job. Do what is necessary to qualify, even if it means shooting for an objective that is a year or two away. See yourself from the perspective of some years from now, and imagine yourself being single forever.

Establish yourself in a role which pleases and extends you and makes you self-sufficient, so if an emotional partner comes along, you have something definite and substantial to offer in terms of your money-making capacities. Don't assume that your partner will have his financial self in any better order than you have yours, and prepare for that probability.

Seek employment where you can advance. Even if you have to start at a low level and to be an apprentice for a while, get into something where you can grow. Invest your time and build a reputation for doing a good job whatever you are doing. Find reasons to excel, go all out, and money will come. Attitude is what is important, and if you feel you *are* your work, that your work is enjoyable at levels beyond the financial, then chances are that you will attract money enough to live and enjoy life.

The most important attitude to maintain and cultivate is a feeling of *Yes, I can.* Yes, you can make money by doing what you want to do. You can find a way to take care of your financial self by taking care of your inner self. Instead of finding reasons why you can't do something, give yourself reasons why you *can.* Make it happen.

So ends the chapter on the Wheel of Fortune. The wheel is really you, which you activate and send out into the world. What meets you there is a matter of destiny and circumstance, but how you meet opportunities depends only on yourself.

The idea that you need a partner to survive is not practical and leads to more trouble than it is worth. The idea that you are responsible for the quality of your life leads to freedom of action and expression.

Everybody is a single, whether he knows it or not. Before you can make it with another person, you have to learn how to make it with yourself. Spinning your Wheel of Fortune with conscious efforts and inputs can take you out of the dark and into the light.

The idea is not whatever will be will be, but whatever you *want* will be.

CHAPTER THREE

Breaking the Ice

It was September in the city, springtime for new love, when a rush of activity blossoms and blooms from the oppressive heat of August. There had been a run of 80-degree days and 60 degree evenings, and the outdoor cafés were open and bustling. Young couples sat sipping sangria and holding hands, discussing what was new and good in town and if Bogdanovich would ever make another decent movie.

Richard Watson was alone on this glorious Thursday afternoon, and he didn't want to be. He had left his past behind, a love-and-hate saga, including a wife, two children and mechanical, steady employment. He preferred to believe that his present condition was simply a matter of circumstance, a sad conclusion of a too-early, sexually centered, parentally conditioned marriage. The divorce was by mutual consent. Now as he cruised the Upper East Side, the thirty-five-year-old and free Mr. Watson looked into the eyes of single women for an invitation to ... to friendship, if nothing else. Richard knew no one in the city, and his freedom was weighing heavily on his head.

Anna Palladino slid into her usual seat at Eric's, a tasteful, warm, informal meeting place across the street from the more famous and ritzy Elaine's. The summer had not been a good one for her. The wealthy man she had been living with had taken sudden leave to Hawaii without a note or phone call of explanation. She packed her bags and decided to be unavailable whenever he came back. Although his leavetaking had occurred at the beginning of the summer, Anna was still in her period of mourning and retreat, scotch and soda her only companion. The regulars around Eric's did not have to be told to stay off Anna's back. But in the recesses of her heart she was expecting the unexpected. She was genuinely available if the right man came along.

So it was on the most instantaneous of impulses that Richard Watson met Anna Palladino. She described herself as having "a great pair of tits," and although she did not go out of her way to display her most generous of physical resources, her open-necked, bare-shouldered, stylish cotton summer dress did most of the advertising for her.

It was about 5:45 P.M. Eric's was cool and quiet, just the way Anna liked it. Richard ordered a Tom Collins, met Anna's eyes and lost control.

"Nice place," he said for openers, unable to ignore her delicate hands, her deeply tanned shoulders and generous, "great pair of tits."

"Not bad," she said with a half-smile, not encouraging or discouraging him.

"They don't have many places like this in Kansas City."

Kansas City, oh, shit, she thought. Then she looked away through the window, pretending to be waiting for somebody.

"No," said Richard, "Kansas City is not New York. No way."

Anna tried to signal the bartender with her eyes, but he was on the phone and could not come to her rescue.

"Say, I'm new in the city, and I'm kinda lost. Do you mind if I ask you a few questions?"

"What kind of questions? The usual questions?"

"I don't know," Richard said, turning toward her with an open smile. "What are the usual questions?"

"First you'll want to know where I work and what I do, then where I live, then if I've got a boyfriend, then if I'd like to go to dinner, then if I'd like to fuck; then you'll probably tell me that you have a wife and two kids back home and just need some tender love and care because you're a thousand miles away from home. You know, the standard Midwestern bullshit."

Richard swallowed and looked down at the bar.

Anna called for her check and walked out of Eric's. Later that night she cried herself to sleep. Later that night Richard got drunk, got lost and thought about going back home to Kansas City.

This story raises some basic questions for the single or recently divorced person wanting to get back into circulation.

What can you do to break the ice in unfamiliar situations?

Where can you go to meet someone you like, respect and feel comfortable with?

How can you cope with your dire need for someone to love and to love you in return?

What can you do to fill the empty spaces and lonely nights of weekends, holidays and time by yourself?

How can you get a handle on your fear of rejection and your need to feel worthy as an individual?

How can you take advantage of being single at your age?

How can you start again after a disappointing love affair and get back into circulation?

Breaking the ice, getting back into circulation, maintaining and sustaining a relationship of depth and meaning are prime concerns for a number of singles in our society—a number which is growing larger every year. Since breaking the ice means learning to give of yourself, it is not something that comes naturally or easily to the majority of single people. Since we have been taught not to give, not to risk, not to express feelings at the outset of a new relationship, breaking the ice really means learning a new set of rules and techniques of human interpersonal behavior. Time after time single people *withdraw* in situations where they could make contact if they had a positive view of themselves as individuals, if they were willing to reach out and touch rather than sit back and wait.

Because living the single life is always full of risks, potentials and excess psychic baggage, the first capacity to be refined is confidence in yourself as an individual. You can meet people anywhere, doing anything, once you have made peace with yourself—the kind of peace that sees risk as an opportunity for growth rather than as a reason to hide. The difficult work starts with a total commitment to yourself in time, energy and effort. Once that is in progress—through the exercises and techniques suggested in the earlier chapters—a second stage begins.

Once you have started your homework and filled in your empty nights with work on yourself, you can then move out into the social world. All work on the self amounts to nothing if you don't go out into the field and play. That's where you risk, take chances and give of yourself. That's where the fun is.

"I wanted love. I wanted to be loved. I wanted somebody to hold me at night and care about how my day went. But I ran away from everyone who offered me unconditional love. When the time came to give of myself totally and completely, all I felt was fear," said a thirty-year-old woman, a teacher of children's dance classes. "I couldn't seem to risk intimacy, even though I thought I wanted it."

Risking intimacy with another person is as frightening as, if not more frightening than, facing yourself and looking into your personal depths, yet both actions must be taken if you are to become truly involved with another human being.

Breaking the ice involves something much deeper than making a first move at a resort poolside or at a company cocktail party. It's much more than having a stock set of lines at hand or being consciously witty to impress a new would-be lover. Breaking the ice and establishing emotional rapport with another human being activate many internal systems because something is at stake—both for you and for the other person.

Richard Watson and Anna Palladino had their hearts encased in ice. Although an opportunity was presented to each of them, both let it slip by because of what they did not do, as well as because of what they in fact did. Both were operating under a certain intellectual and emotional fantasy and did not see themselves or the other clearly.

There are some basic rules for breaking the ice with another human being, both at the first encounter and in the developing relationship. The "rules" are not easy to discern, much less to follow, because they are not set and rigid. Yet when they are kept in mind and adapted to your individual style, they seem to ease the fear of rejection and raise the level of confidence. They make it easier for you to meet people wherever you go because they give you something to do under all conditions.

Give Yourself a Psychological Game Plan—A Task

When Richard Watson wandered into Eric's and encountered Anna Palladino, he had no *ideas* behind his actions. He was operating on pure chance, driven by an impulse, unsure of where he was or of what he wanted. He felt himself to be in a kind of twilight zone, and breaking the ice under those conditions is just about impossible.

Without a psychological game plan in mind, Richard was at the mercy of circumstances. When he saw Anna and reacted viscerally to her stunning feminine charms, his eyes glazed over and his heart began to beat. All ideas went out the window, and he came off as dull, boring and obvious. He was there but not quite "there." His behavior was that of a man acting out a scene he had imagined in a fantasy years before.

Richard had no *task* in mind. He was not conscious of what he was *doing* above and beyond what he was saying. Therefore, his behavior was inappropriate to the situation and to the woman sitting next to him. He had nothing really to say because he had nothing really to do. He was not acting on any set of ideas, and he was definitely not being himself. He forced his behavior; he forced the conversation; he tried to force Anna to react to him, even though she did not want to.

It is important to have an idea when you are in a situation where you don't know anyone but would like to meet someone. One of the most useful concepts in such unfamiliar, possibly threatening situations is that of a task—giving yourself something to do and something to keep in mind that take away the nervousness of the moment.

A simple illustration of a task has been demonstrated vividly on many occasions in the Hunter singles class. As an experiment, I would ask a volunteer simply to stand in front of the room facing the entire group, just to stand for a minute, without doing or saying anything. *Every* volunteer squirmed, shuffled and became flushed, feeling very uncomfortable. Standing there, doing nothing, in front of unknown people was like being tossed totally naked into a fishbowl.

After thirty seconds or so I would take the volunteer aside and ask her—usually the person was a female since women have, as a rule, much more courage than men—to count the people in the room, registering the number of men and women. As soon as the person had a task, something to do, all the nervous mannerisms began to disappear. Once she was engaged in an activity—a mental, psychic activity—her behavior changed noticeably. Every volunteer was more relaxed, more at ease, more herself.

In some ways the idea of a task, of giving yourself something to do and to accomplish, seems very obvious and simplistic. Yet when asked if they had given themselves a task for the day or for the meeting, most people in the Hunter singles class said no. In fact, most had no conscious idea of why there were sitting in the singles meeting. They came out of curiosity and just sat there, waiting to see what would happen, more ready to *react* than to take a chance.

This psychological posture is widespread and deadly to any creative use of individual potentials. Without a conscious idea of *doing something* in a new and unfamiliar situation, people allow events to control them. They are at the mercy of the elements because they themselves put nothing into it but hope, fear and anxiety.

But giving yourself a mental task changes the flow of the energy. You can project something of yourself into the situation. Instead of negatively allowing circumstance to reduce you into forced, contrived and obvious behavior, you can color the circumstance with your own thinking, feeling and willing.

Keeping a task in mind can help you change the negative to the positive.

Following are some practical, useful and very powerful tasks to try when you know you are going to be in a situation where you would like to break the ice.

HAVE A GOOD TIME

As strange as it may seem, many single people are psychologically keyed to finding the negative in every person they meet and in every place they go. They are primed toward criticism because they carry around with them negative past experiences and ideas of how other people should be. They wonder if the perfect mate will suddenly appear tonight. They worry about how they look and if other people will want them. They don't know what they will say or how to react. They allow the anxiety of the past to follow them into the present. They fall victims to their own insecurities and past failures. The saddest thing of all is that for many people these negative thought patterns exist at a subconscious level. They are not aware of how negative they really are.

Yet the task of having a good time can overcome these fears and anxieties. It doesn't matter if your boyfriend left you last month for another woman. It doesn't matter if the woman you love is in love with someone else. The past does not *have* to get in the way if you give yourself something conscious and positive to do in the moment.

One thirty-two-year-old schoolteacher from Brooklyn, a woman with a history of many short-lived love affairs, reported that when she told herself to have a good time and enjoy the new situation, the pressure of having to find a special man was reduced. She had never given herself the game plan of having a good time or enjoying the moment before. She had always felt she had to meet somebody who wanted her *that night.*

To her, having a good time meant dancing and talking to several people. From the moment she began to dress for the evening until the moment she left the party, she concerned herself with having a good time. She projected a positive energy from within herself to other people. Giving *herself* something to do mentally changed her behavior and lowered the pressure level.

After practicing the idea of a task on several different occasions—a public social affair, a party at a friend's house, a weekend on the shore, a business luncheon—she felt more comfortable with herself and was less threatened by new people or new situations than she had been. She was freer to take a chance and not to wait for another person to make a first move.

She was "working" on her task but had never had such a good time.

CHANGE THE NEGATIVE TO THE POSITIVE

Many single people are victims of their own prejudices and prejudgments. On many occasions I have witnessed both men and women attend a singles function, take one walk around the room, turn and leave, thinking that "there is no one here for me." They carry around with them a preconceived ideal of the perfect mate, and when the ideal does not jump out at them in the first few minutes, they are ready to turn tail and run.

One young lawyer in the Hunter class testified that he had lived with eight models in five years. A graduate of Dartmouth, the Harvard School of Business and the London School of Economics, he was well dressed, articulate and obviously a man-on-the-go. But he had an idea in mind—a model for a mate—that simply did not work for him. He refused to pay attention to his track record. He refused to alter his idea of what he wanted in a woman. He wanted someone who looked striking, but he did not realize that the inner life was ultimately more important than any physical look or style.

Changing the negative to the positive is a task which can be kept in mind in any new situation. Even if no one person attracts you physically, a good exercise is to make contact with someone intellectually or emotionally. The young lion of a lawyer missed the opportunity of meeting some interesting women because he ran away so quickly. If he had stayed, he could have developed friendships which might have eased his loneliness and altered his model archetype.

Changing the negative to the positive has several planes of action: It means changing your negative attitude about yourself, as well as your negative attitude about others.

Instead of casting judgments and making decisions about other people in a room, try to find the positive. Try to make another person feel good by showing interest or concern. This does not mean that you have to stay with that person all night.

But the idea of going into a party, class or business function consciously attempting to change the negative to the positive builds up a very real quality of confidence when it is practiced regularly. The idea has a force behind it, a guiding principle.

A majority of single people do not have a positive idea when they go out to break the ice. Therefore, anyone who *does* have an idea in mind—a task he is performing—stands out from the rest.

OBSERVE IN DETAIL

A good objective in all new situations is to observe the behavior of other people *in detail* and *without judgment.* Transform yourself into a sensitive receiver, and tune into the inner currents of other people, places and situations. By doing so, you become better able to discern when to make a move and when to stay in a holding pattern. Timing is all-important, and knowing when to make a move is essential in the ice-melting process. As you learn to distinguish between the receptive person and the one who is likely to reject you, you are, in fact, preparing yourself for a relationship of quality and depth.

Certain qualities to look for when you observe in detail may be called the vital signs. You may have some of your own to add to this list, but these can provide a beginning.

THE SEVEN VITAL SIGNS

1. Look for the difference between what a person says and what he does. Does he practice what he preaches? What is the difference between the way he is and the way he wants to be?

2. Look at whether a person takes care of himself or neglects himself. Look at the condition of his body, his clothes and the way he carries himself. Look for the inner self-image, compared to the outer wrapping of the package.

3. Look for intentions and objectives behind words and actions. Does the person have an idea of what he is doing, or is his behavior arbitrary, tentative and unspecific?

4. Look for a connection between words and feelings. Are the words attached to or detached from emotions? Is the person centered in his head, heart or genitals? What is the ruling organ?

5. Look for the daily and the ultimate task of the person. Is there a conscious attempt at growth and self-development, or is he just going through the motions of living? What is he working for, and why?

6. Look for prejudices and tastes in behavior. Examine what the person values by what he does. Look for his stumbling blocks, blind spots *and* virtues.

7. Look for a harmony within the person. Is there a connection between the inner and the outer selves? At what stage of development are his thinking, feeling and willing powers?

As you look for these qualities in others, turn the camera in on yourself to check your own vital signs. How do you stand up to these same questions? How do you appear to other people?

Avoid High-Risk Situations

A high-risk situation is one where there is pressure to make contact immediately. Pickup places, singles bars, beaches, dances, parties often create an atmosphere or condition where singles are not themselves. In such situations people say and do things which are forced, superficial and inconsequential. There is often a flurry of activity, a casual exchange of platitudes and a quick, depressing exit or the meaninglessness of a one-night stand.

Most lasting relationships—friendships and romances—begin under conditions where there is little pressure to meet somebody and where there is a *shared activity.* People meet people when they aren't trying to meet people but are in the process of learning or enjoying themselves.

From 65 to 70 percent of meaningful, long-lasting relationships grow out of attending a class, meeting at work or participating in neighborhood situations. People meet each other while engaged in an activity where they come into

contact with others on *more than one occasion*. When there are
a series of meetings, people are able to melt the ice instead of
having to break it. Relationships have a chance to grow at a
mellow pace rather than at a hit-or-miss, all-or-nothing shoot-
out.

Melting the ice is a potent weapon against the fear of
rejection. The very idea takes away some of the psychological
pressure of having to meet someone *now*. Once you slow down
and begin to relax and enjoy, emotions, ideas and laughter
begin to flow more smoothly.

You don't have to be witty, charming, macho or demure.
All you have to do is be yourself and let things happen rather
than force them to.

Take the Time to Relax and Get to Know the Other Person

Relaxation is the key to overcoming the fear of rejection. If
you can relax under pressure, chances are you will be more
willing and able to make a move toward another person when
the time is right.

Everyone is more himself or herself when relaxed and at
ease, but there is something even more important at stake.
When you know how to relax, the other person will also be
more relaxed and open. When you are relaxed, you have
greater psychological perception into the inner activities of the
other person.

Single people seem to agree that the most seductive quality
one may have is psychological perception—an ability to see
and to sense the undercurrents of character or the invisible
actions of a situation. Relaxation makes you more perceptive,
more attuned to the needs of the other person so that you can
relate better to the other as an individual.

Many times a single person has in his head an ideal of what
is right, cool, proper. Then, when the situation arises, the
person will live out his idea of should-be-done, the idea of
what is sexy, witty, charming, etc.

Sometimes the best thing to do is to do nothing at all. Nothing, that is, except relax, enjoy and get to know the other person. Love cannot be forced or coerced. It must be given freely, or it soon withers and dies on the vine. Willingness on your part to get to know the other person, to allow emotions to flow is a signal of your own sophistication and character.

Practicing relaxation and taking time are a very solid investment.

Shared Learning Experience

Going out and doing things is not enough.

One single man went to five or six events a week at different clubs and organizations and just sat on the sidelines and watched. He went but did not participate and suffered the illusion of action. Sometimes keeping busy is merely a camouflage for fear and insecurity.

Keeping active counts, but what you do and how you do it are even more important. One of the best ways to develop confidence, refine talents and meet people at the same time is the shared learning experience. This consists of deliberately placing yourself under conditions of growth and learning with others who are also learning. In a sense, you seek your own level of competence, which puts everybody in the same boat. Then the activity of learning will bring you together with other people of the same mind and the same heart.

The shared learning experience is an active rather than a passive event. Taking classes that require some kind of participation provides the most positive arena for growth. A class which somehow asks you and every member of the group to *perform* usually helps you make the most friends.

For example, an acting class which studies behavior and asks the participant to get onstage is better than a lecture class on Renaissance painting. A photography class in which projects are to be completed in the "real" world is better for meeting people than a literature class which keeps you home alone reading. A music class where you are learning to play an instrument by practicing is better than any class which simply reinforces what you already know.

The quality of the class draws a certain quality of person, and the activity which has participation built into its conceptual fabric always spawns new friendships. In acting class you have to rehearse with a partner. In photography class you must sharpen your eye to the form, content and composition of the outer world. Learning music will give you an outlet and something to do to fill the spaces of weekends and holidays.

Just reading or studying is not enough. These acts can isolate a person in an illusory bubble of well-being. Acting, participating, sharing new experiences with other people— these build relationships without much effort. A shared learning experience takes time, an investment of more than one night.

Taking a class that meets eight, ten or twelve times gives you something to look forward to. It offers people, action and talk about what is happening to each and every individual. Learning more about yourself and about others can be the best kind of recreation. It builds and refines psychological perception and awareness on the deeper levels of experience.

Continuing education for the adult person is now a booming business all over the country, an industry which will be growing and spreading to all areas. In the effort to extend yourself, chances are very good that you will meet someone else with similar needs, interests and desires.

Don't Rush or Expect Sex Immediately

One of the most common complaints from single women of all ages is that men want to go to bed right away. If a woman declines his offer, the man usually reels from the blow to his masculine ego and simply never calls again. Somehow sex is the bottom line for a great number of single men. Everything else in a relationship is incidental and superfluous.

Rushing to sex is perhaps the best way to guarantee a life of being single for a long time. Even with the pill and modern means of contraception, sex is a more delicate, private event for many women than it is for men—more emotional, more precious, more personal.

One forty-five-year-old public relations man reported an incident which puzzled and stung him deeply. He was an articulate, nice-looking man, but one who wanted sexual, emotional contact immediately. At a party he met an attractive forty-year-old woman. After a few drinks and laughs she invited him over to her house for dinner the following evening. Taking this as a cue that she "wanted some action," he began pawing her arm, her knee, her shoulder.

Feeling that there was "not much time," he made a pass at her which she sidestepped neatly. The next morning she called him, quite upset, to withdraw the invitation to dinner. She accused him of lunging at her, and under no conditions did she want a lunger. He was confused and hurt. He had no idea of what he had done wrong, and rather than look to himself for the responsibility, he attacked the woman for her immaturity and inability to face "reality."

The mistake this man made was to impose his own time pressure on the woman. He would have come closer to what he wanted if he had stepped back, looking for ways to become aware of *her* sensibilities. His own magic formula of one evening's talk and laughter was not enough for her. And for many women.

Being attractive, sociable and sensitive, she was the target of many come-ons, so someone who did *not* come on—someone who took the time to understand her as a person—had a better chance of starting a relationship.

Expecting sex immediately puts pressure on both the new partners. Sex carries a weight which is anything but casual, a weight that grows heavier as a person grows older. When young, a person can be cavalier about sex, interested in numbers and quick getaways. But as one grows older, more is at stake with sex, something deeper of the self, and it pays not to rush or expect sex too quickly or too easily.

The physical act of sex is satisfying only when there is an emotional and spiritual foundation. Entering the body of another human being activates many psychic and unconscious systems, so it is best to take time, make emotional investments and offer sex—gently and quietly—rather than to force or demand it.

Let it be given as a gift, an exchange of two willing hearts.

Pay Attention to the Unexpected

A number of single men and women report that love walked into their lives when they least expected it. Somehow the trick is *not* to look for love, *not* to search for someone special, *not* to scan faces in the crowd, waiting for bells to ring and gongs to sound.

Although there is a psychological and emotional preparation within the individual which he or she can affect consciously, very often the key event or situation comes about *unexpectedly*. Almost as if by chance. As if by fate. By Coincidence.

There are certain events which you can control. You can eat right, exercise, put your house in order, refine your thinking, feeling and willings. But other events that come to you from the outside will be turning points or opportunities. Unfortunately these opportunities are missed by a great number of single people because of their idea that the unexpected is trivial or insignificant. They do not know what to follow up and what to ignore. Because the unexpected is new, people often shy away from it. Because it is unknown, it is threatening.

But more often than not the unexpected telephone call, invitation, change of job or address is a signal that something important is happening on the psychic plane. In effect, the psyche is calling for new input to alter the familiar pattern of action. When the inner life is ready and poised for action, there inevitably comes something (or someone) from the outside to stimulate or to test the individual at all levels.

It takes a certain kind of training and refined perception to spot the importance of the unexpected event at the moment it occurs. But the general rule of thumb is to begin to pay careful attention to the small unexpected events of daily life: a smile from someone who is usually staid and withdrawn; a kind word from a neighbor who is usually deaf and dumb; a gesture from a colleague who is usually wrapped up in himself. The awareness of small, delicate, almost imperceptible events builds a capacity to see more deeply into the obvious unexpected events.

A profitable and intriguing practice is to jot down the unexpected events of each day in your personal inventory journal. If you are like most people, you will begin to perceive a pattern even in those events which will give you a clue to when to make a move and when to sit back and wait. Insight into the unexpected events of your life can lead to an intuitive knowledge of *timing*. Instead of becoming agitated that nothing is happening and the future looks bleak, awareness of your own internal rhythms can reduce anxiety about being single.

Be Yourself

A surprising number of single people are not happy with themselves and the course of their lives. Being single is a constant source of tension, a mark that somehow they are not good or worthy as human beings. They try to impress others. They wear masks, change costumes and pretend to be what they would like to be.

Yet the best way to impress somebody is not to try to

impress. Especially in a situation where single people meet, one of the best efforts to make is to be yourself. If you feel yourself pushing, forcing or somehow being at odds with the situation, you will have a very difficult time breaking the ice or overcoming your shyness.

The best way to be yourself and overcome shyness is to create conditions where you feel relaxed and at home with yourself. A step-by-step procedure which you can follow and fall into with your personal style has proved effective for those who have the vision and perspective to carry it out to the end.

There are four phases in starting to develop a stable relationship. Each phase takes time, It is possible to go through each phase in one night. But the procedure works better when more time is invested than when there is a rush to completion.

Phase One consists of placing yourself in a situation where you *enjoy* your activity. It could be a local theatrical group, or a political organizational rally, or a neighborhood social event, like a block party, holiday festival or cocktails at friends' homes. The idea is that there is some activity going on so that you don't have to stand around and wait, feeling out of place.

This first phase should also occur in some *neutral space,* a space which you can leave by yourself at any time whenever you feel like it. The neutrality of the space ensures an easy exit if you are uncomfortable or if you are cornered by someone who doesn't capture your eye, head or heart. Ideally this neutral space is one where you can return more than once. The activity is somehow ongoing, always *there* when you want it to be there.

Your task in this neutral public place is to have some coffee or exchange a phone number and to offer a meeting on some other, more personal ground. This offer should not occur immediately. Dates should first be made in the neutral public space, and time should be invested. No rush, no push. Get to know without demands, contracts or expectations. Go three or four times. Find out if there is anybody there you want to see again, genuinely want to see again.

If so, go back and relate your feelings to the person you want to see again. Take the chance. Make the move. Communicate your ideas, feelings and intuitions. That is your first task.

Make an effort to go back at least a few times before making judgments on the quality of the people there.

Phase Two of the operation starts in a public but more personal place—like a park, a restaurant or a concert hall. It should be some place where there is still an activity to be shared, but which allows for a more one-on-one, individual exchange. The task in some ways remains the same: to take the time to get to know the other person. Find out likes and dislikes. Ask the person to talk about favorite songs, influential people, memorable events.

A good topic for conversation is what was happening to each of you ten years before. Try to recapture the specific time, place and situation. What songs did you like, what was happening in your life, were you in love, how have your ideas about love changed in these ten years?

The task in this second phase is to relax with the other person and talk about both your histories. Create the atmosphere within yourself of being a good listener; this means listening in silence and listening without criticism.

In this public, yet personal space, receive information about the other person's internal life and psychic history. Be willing to reveal feelings, episodes and occasions of the past honestly and directly. Don't wait for the other person to do it, but *offer* to give of yourself first.

If nothing happens or the rendezvous simply peters out, all you have lost is some time. Neither you nor the other person is locked in by a too-soon, casual sexual encounter, and it is relatively easy to go your own way.

But if you still want more of the person, if he or she is on your mind at odd times during the day and dreamy times at night, take another step closer. Phase Three.

Invite the person into your private place, your home. Share a dinner; make it together; clean up together; be together for the entire evening. But the one who has come into the house expects to leave. Make it clear that this third phase includes sleeping in separate quarters—*especially* if you feel warm, healthy and attached to the other person.

Phase Three consciously and deliberately has no sleeping-together expectations. Find out (if you can) about the most recent love affair of this person. How did it take shape; how did it end; did it end at all emotionally?

Even in Phase Three many singles wear masks, preferring not to reveal the *last* emotional involvement because they cannot quite let it go. The last affair has a nasty habit of lingering on disguised as enthusiasm and need, but very often you may simply be a substitute, a standby, an understudy for the "real love" of the other person's life.

Phase Three is subtle and dangerous. Something starts to be at stake here, something volatile and emotional. It is an extremely delicate phase, one that is often skipped over because the delights of the bedroom are just on the other side of the wall. The task here is to get a clear reading about the head and the heart of the other person *before* you go poking around between the legs.

The last thing you do is invite somebody into your body. You invite someone into your bed to exchange juices and energies because the two of you are *better* than one. Each of you has retained the precious and necessary gift of individuality, but you have also given and invested something of yourself which makes you feel a part of the other.

Phase Four brings sexual love with commitment and caring—the kind of sexual exchange which binds souls together in a magical, mysterious way. If either of the two partners is using the other, experimenting as it were, not "there" all the way, pulling back at the last moment, the sexual exchange is premature, frustrating and potentially dangerous.

Because sex is so available, used for recreational purposes, Phase Four is often fraught with confusion, bitterness and anger. Sleeping with or not sleeping with is often a tumultuous scene, one that will be more carefully examined in Chapter Seven.

The idea is to break the ice—or, rather, to melt the ice.

It always comes down to taking the chance to give of yourself. Create the conditions where you are sharing an activity. Make the effort to go back to a particular place more than once. Take the time to get to know the person as an individual. Deliberately take time, and don't rush yourself or the other person.

Allow the ice to melt around the heart.

Perhaps your gentleness and understanding is the greatest gift you can give.

CHAPTER FOUR

Roles and Scenes

Once upon a time, when male and female roles were more strictly defined and were lived up to as a matter of tradition, being single was a clear-cut role to play. Either the single person was a free spirit and a creative artist who blazed his own trail in a fiery rebellion against the insipid bourgeois values or he was an eccentric neurotic who couldn't give anything of himself to another person. There were nutty bachelors and prunelike old maids. Thank God there were more normal couples with families and responsibilities to keep the world and the country rolling smoothly.

But these days the role of being single is not clearly defined because more and more people are seeking to define and refine themselves as individuals first. With more educational, social and business opportunities available, both men and women are facing the questions and challenges of self-identity *before* they sign a lifelong contract with another human being. But in the process of finding oneself and developing one's talents, there is the question of what rules and standards are to replace the old ones.

What does a single person have to live up to?

What are the rules of the game for a single man and woman? What are the standards, expectations and obligations involved when one flies solo? What are the demands one is to place on oneself and then on other people?

What, in short, is the role of being single?

A major difference between being coupled and being single is that, being single, one is "allowed" to have more than one relationship. There are many people to love, with whom to share time, space and energy. Since there is no exclusive contract, it is not only possible but also advantageous to spice one's life with a variety of psychic and physical bodies. Loving several people at one time is part of the game plan. The "rules" allow for more than one.

But those rules turn in and against a person. The more-than-one rule is difficult, disturbing and distracting to live up to.

Mary L. is now a thirty-seven-year-old divorcée, who separated from her husband in 1967 when she was twenty-eight. She felt that she had married too soon because of her fear of being alone the rest of her life. But when she had been married for several years, she felt she was missing much of what the world had to offer. Being a woman of independent means, she was able to afford to travel all over the globe to satisfy her curious mind and her thirst for action. She began a lively search for the right man which took her into the arms of a famous Italian film director, a world champion bridge player, a shifty Scorpion poet and other assorted soldiers of fortune.

At the age of thirty-three, she settled in with a professional gambler, a staid and withdrawn cardplayer who had a computer for a mind and who played everything with the best odds. He would rise out of bed at about ten in the morning, watch some game shows on TV, go to the bridge club about noon, play until six or seven, then head to dinner with $100 in his pocket. On an average $600 a week.

In this particular relationship Mary laid out the rules. Each was to be free to see and sleep with other people. They would keep separate places of residence. There would be dinners, weekends and shared vacations, plans made with and for each other. At first the gambler wasn't comfortable with Mary's need to be free, but soon he began to make the shift from his mental objections to an openness in his heart. The time with Mary was for him warm, humorous and intellectually stimulating. She made him feel wanted, needed and appreciated, yet there was something not quite right.

He wanted her more than she wanted him, so she had the power in the relationship. On several occasions when he wanted to be with her, she would be off with her other "friends." She had her other "needs," and *he* had to make the adjustments. It took awhile—almost two years—but the gambler began to trust her and play by her rules of the game.

Then, one Wednesday night, the gambler called Mary and asked to have dinner with her in such a tone of voice that a shiver went through her body. He would not go into details on the phone, and in the time she waited for him to arrive, Mary had a fit of solar plexus feelings. Gut flinchings. Flashes of fear. High anxiety ripples.

Sure enough, when the gambler came in, he told her he was going away for the weekend with another woman. Because he was so cautious and deliberate, because he always checked the consequences *before* he made a move, because all his actions had a weight and a meaning behind them, Mary was crushed. Her own brief excursions into sex and pleasure with other people had been feathery and weightless, mere distractions and titillations. They meant nothing. She had simply wanted to keep her options open.

Now the rules rebounded against her. In that one moment, when he told her he was going away with another woman, something broke forever in Mary's heart: trust; confidence; openness. She felt hurt, rejected, unwanted. Slowly Mary and her gambler drifted apart. He would call wanting to see her, but her vision of him with another woman was too painful for her to endure. He was not "hers" anymore. Emotionally she could not share him, even though conceptually she could. The rules she had written were not working to her advantage, so she stopped playing completely.

The pain of being single was the pain of being alone, unwanted and left for another woman. She had built up a certain strength and self-sufficiency as a "single," but being alone was not the same thing as being single. Being single was playing the game to her advantage with other people, but being alone was playing no game to no advantage.

Mary began to hurt. She had no handle on her pain. She didn't know where to turn, what to do or where to meet new people. Hers was the ache of wanting someone to want her but having no one there. She had constructed rules in her head that did not have a place in her heart, so she remained sore, rejected, unloved and unwanted.

Until she turned on some of her "liberated" guns.

Being single, unattached and available, feeling the emptiness of the seven-thirty-to-bedtime weekday blues, Mary decided to take control of her life by playing the aggressor. Her most acute pain was her fear of tomorrow, so she set out to get what she wanted instead of playing the waiting game.

In her neighborhood pharmacy there was a young man who worked nights while going to graduate school during the days. After a few prescriptions and several tubes of toothpaste, Mary invited the lean and lanky young man to stop by to see her after work. Although he was fifteen years her junior, she wanted him to want her. She offered, in her subtle and charming way, to initiate him into the ecstatic delights of a warm and loving relationship with a good woman.

After a few cautious evenings of talk, pot and yoga-exercises, the young pharmacist stayed overnight. He was attentive, innocent and passionate. He left in the morning, smiling and happy, vowing to see her again soon.

He didn't call for three days. Three days and three nights she waited, observing the higher spiritual principle of allowing the other person freedom of choice and action. Three days and three nights she suffered. She thought about calling him. She thought about not calling him. She thought about *not* not calling him. She thought about making a fool of herself. Then she thought about the risk factor in all emotional and psychic enlightenment.

About midnight of the third day she picked up the phone on impulse and called him with the intention of finding out where he stood "once and for all." She knew it was not fair to force him into an action, but she wanted to *know*. She wanted him to miss, appreciate and love her all the more because of the three-day separation. She wanted him to feel the way she felt.

The telephone rang just once. He picked it up almost as if he were expecting the call.

"Hi, Marty. It's Mary."

There was a short but seemingly tumultuous pause at the other end of the line.

"Hi, how are you?" he asked in a dull, flat, disappointed tone.

That was his answer to her wants, needs and fantasies. In that one flashing, unrehearsed, spontaneous moment she saw that he didn't want her, that he didn't care enough to call and that his orbit was on a totally different plane from hers.

His "Hi, how are you?" was a punch in the gut. As the confessed and conscious aggressor she had put herself on the line. She hadn't got him the *way* she wanted him, so she felt the pain. She herself had created the conditions of the rejection that provoked her own pain. The pain of being alone was bad, but the pain of being in a one-sided relationship was much worse.

She had activated her own human, personal, individual powers of freedom to initiate an action. Then she had to absorb the emotional consequences of that action. He "kind of, sort of, once in a while" wanted to be with her, but he didn't have the guts or the presence of mind to tell her so.

That was unsatisfactory to Mary, so she found herself back at square one.

She had married more or less unconsciously and had turned away from that. She had chosen adventure and a series of affairs and had turned away from that. She had played by the rules of her own making and had turned away from that. She had initiated an aggressive action and had turned away from that.

What next? she thought.

She still ached to be wanted. She wanted someone to need her and find her attractive. She had experienced the pain of coming together and breaking up, and now she didn't have time for the pain.

Where could she turn? What could she do?

Mary did what many nice, conservative, responsible, cautious, semidesperate women of comfortable means fail to do. She turned into herself with the assumption that something *she* was doing was determining the quality of her relationships with men. By sitting down with her journal in a relaxed, objective way, writing the story of her ten most important heterosexual relationships, she discovered that:

1. She had married because she *expected* that her husband would take care of her and complete her life. Her husband had wanted and pursued her. She had defined herself in terms of his want and his need. She had been a function of him.
2. After her separation she had sought adventurous affairs because she had *expected* to find the right man in exotic places. In the name of liberation.
3. She had then sought an open relationship because she had *expected* the intellectual rules of mutual freedom to work to her advantage all the time, every time.
4. She had sought an affair with a younger man and had *expected* him to recognize her warmth and loving

nature immediately, thereby satisfying her own fading ego.

By writing down the essential action of each of her major romantic affairs in her journal, she saw that her own expectations always got in her way. Her personal, individual set of expectations always involved some kind of emotional obligation from her partner—where he would *have to* complete or make her life important.

Expecting fulfillment to come from an outside source, she would go out of her way to live up to her concept that she, as a woman, needed a man to make her life meaningful. It dawned on her, after she had taken the inventory of her personal history, that she *herself* was responsible for her pattern of emotional frustration and social isolation. Nobody was doing *it* to her. She was doing *it* to herself in a very basic, elemental way. She saw that every meeting with someone else was in essence a meeting with herself.

Her own concepts of what should be done had colored every interaction with a man, though she was not aware of it at the time it was happening. She continually played out ideas that did not work for her, ideas that kept her on the surface of love. It seemed that she had acquired some core beliefs, some fixed concepts, some romantic notions from her family, from her education and from her society that not only limited her but also subjected her to a repetitious pattern of frustration.

Mary came to realize that most of her affairs with men were based on personal gratification and sexual contentment. Her actions had a undercurrent of self-gratification and egoistic pleasure. Even her giving had an unconscious motive of self-gratification underneath, so that in a very subtle way all her actions depended on another person for completion. She placed herself at the mercy of the other person—usually a man—all the time. *Her internal computer was somehow programming her own singleness,* even though she did not want to be single, on a conscious level.

She came to this somewhat surprising conclusion by making a list of core concepts. It might be useful and instructive for you to follow her lead by taking a similar profile inventory in your own journal.

A core concept is something that you implicitly believe is true for you. It is a belief you have learned and ingested so that it is now a part of your psychic bloodstream. You carry this core concept with you wherever you go, and your "natural," instinctive reactions are based on this invisible, often unconscious mind set to outer events.

For example, what are your core concepts or beliefs about:

1. The right man?

2. The ideal woman?

3. Your parents, separately and together?

4. Your work (what are you working for)?

5. God or divine forces?

6. Sex?

7. Yourself?

8. Yourself ten years from today?

How do your answers to these core concepts affect your daily life and your relationship with yourself?

Do you, for example, believe that you have control over the quality of your life? If not, chances are that events will conspire against you.

Do you tend to blame or criticize other people or circumstances for your present state of mind, either positive or negative? If so, you are putting yourself at the mercy of those people and those circumstances.

Do you have a specific purpose and a specific future goal that can be achieved through your efforts and talents alone, one which does not fundamentally depend on another for completion? If not, your fears of rejection, your fears of being alone and your fears of dying are probably very acute.

Being extremely perceptive, objective and demanding of herself, Mary saw in the personal inventory of her journal that she had been a consumer all her life. She had been taught, encouraged and rewarded to *take* without risking or developing anything of herself. She *expected* life to offer her love, happiness and good fortune as a matter of course. Her actions had been based on a set of expectations which placed a premium on other people and outside forces rather than on herself. She had been taught to depend on other people rather than on her own inner resources. She blindly made an emotional investment based on her complex set of expectations, then paid a vicious psychic price when these expectations were not fulfilled.

Mary then made an emotional, intellectual and spiritual commitment to a course of study and personal development—hers happened to be chemistry—which demanded of her a daily discipline and a sense of service to other people. She went back to school to fill out some basic science requirements. After two years she was accepted into a PhD program and was offered a graduate teaching fellowship. She felt very strongly that *she* had to rearrange her early concepts and her present priorities. Only by consciously forsaking her consumer pattern of behavior could she make the most out of her talents and her life as a single woman.

At that stage in her life—about thirty-five years of age—Mary came to redefine her role as a single woman. Instead of desperately searching for the right man, she turned inward to develop her own *creative* capacities, even though she knew she was getting a late start.

The most important work was work on herself, work she had neglected for many years, thinking that someday the right man would just come along. The work on herself was of a psychic, conceptual nature. She began to put aside personal pleasures and momentary gratifications for the pursuit of knowledge and her own relationship with herself. She consciously set about "to put my own house in order," which meant letting go of things, ideas and people that had meant everything to her in her formative years.

"My greatest challenge is consistently with myself," Mary now says, speaking in the present tense with deliberate purpose. "I believe that I'm single for a reason, and that reason is to let go of the idea that I *should be* married. That I *should* be part of a couple, with children and a house in the suburbs. That I *should* be part of the mainstream.

"I honestly feel that I am working out my own destiny for myself—*that* is what I am supposed to do with my life now. I am single. I have been married. I have had lovers. Now I am left with myself. Now I am to face myself without cringing or apologizing for what might have been. It's frightening to see myself in an emotional mirror, but I intuitively sense that no progress will be made until I can resolve my own relationship with myself, until I can put my expectations to rest and really learn how to take care of myself."

Mary is prepared to live single the rest of her life, which does not mean she has adopted a hermit's robe or placed herself in solitary confinement. Quite the opposite. She has taken responsibility for a women's consciousness-raising group. She rents a share in a summer house on the seashore with a group of professional men and woman. She keeps in touch with friends about the details and events of their lives. After her work, there are parties, vacations and dinners.

But she has consciously removed from her mind and her heart the pressure of finding the right man by giving herself something to do and something to accomplish with her time. Developing a professional talent now is of the prime importance in her life. By making disciplined demands on herself, she finds herself expecting only the unexpected. Now she is more willing and able to take risks, more willing and able to express what she feels and thinks, more ready to be herself under all conditions.

Being yourself is the primary role of being single. To grow as a human being. To make peace with yourself. To understand that no other person can make life complete and happy. To act on the idea that each individual is responsible for his or her own destiny. To accept and to love yourself as an individual first.

We cannot control external circumstances. But we can come to control and color our inner responses to those circumstances. Often the worst part about being single is the *idea* of being single, the idea that one should be coupled, the idea that the later years will be terribly lonely if there is no mate.

If you believe and incorporate these negative ideas into the psychic bloodstream, then those ideas will come into being. If, however, you see the experience of being single as the chance to be free and autonomous, there will be lifelong involvements with people, places, ideas that will fill all the empty gaps.

Mary was sick and tired of being single, deadly afraid of rejection, willing to make concessions and contortions to please a man. Most of all, she wanted to be wanted. But that idea and image of herself only put her at the mercy of that hypothetical man out there. She gave up her freedom and sense of self-reliance; this reduced her to a constant state of anxiety.

The final rejection of the young lover caused her to face herself once and for all. Luckily she had the resources, intelligence and awareness that her past history was going to be repeated and repeated until she changed her attitudes toward herself and being single.

Once she accepted the fact that she controlled the quality of her life and that she did not *need* someone else to make her life whole, she became much happier with herself. Once that happened, she was able to relax, do her work and relate to men as people and friends rather than as lovers or saviors. That change of mind—the transformation of her thinking—had positive results within her entire system.

Facing herself, her ideas about men and her romantic track record made Mary a stronger person. The separation from her husband, her exotic lovers, her stable lover and, finally, her much younger lover made adamant demands on her inner capacities for self-knowledge, self-determination and self-survival. All these affairs made her face herself and her prime responsibility to herself.

Once she accepted that, she began to make the most out of her time and her talents. The idea of being single and needing a man had prevented her from growing, and she was sensitive enough to see that nobody else was doing *it* to her—she was doing *it* to herself.

The role of being single extends far beyond sexual lines. No longer is it relevant to consider what it means to be a *man* or a *woman*. The biological and social differences are not as important as the fact that there is a human ego evolving in each one of us. There is an inner logic to why we are who we are, and often the deeper psyche is much wiser and on target than we are consciously.

Learning how to make peace with your inner self about the condition of being single is the primary lesson to learn. As you put old ideas to sleep and come into your own as an individual, you will find that being single allows you to experience the world and yourself in a way that is unavailable to anyone married or coupled.

Whether it is better or worse than being married or coupled is not the question. It is different—in tone, quality and experience. The paradox is that by accepting your singleness and your individuality, you are closer to making intimate contacts with the external world. The real battleground lies within. Lovers may come and go. Friends may fade away into memories. Families will pass over the threshold into other realms of being.

But there is one relationship that will always be there for you: your relationship with yourself. When the pleasures of the body and the adventure of personal freedom run cold and dry, when loneliness clouds every day with despair, when being single and responsible only to yourself seems a little too much to take, you as a single person need to reach down and tap the creative juices within.

Creativity is the answer. The creative reservoir is inside every one of us. When the outside world is bleak and gray, the inner world is rich and colorful. The inner, creative psyche asks to be used, begs to be awakened, wants to be tapped.

In my own experiences over the years in the Hunter class and in my own travels as a single man, I have come to realize that some people are *supposed* to be single. As if there were an internal computer operating under a higher program, most single people I met were single because they had to face themselves as individuals and learn to live with their choices, dreams and wishes.

There is something strange about being single, something happening within us that barely surfaces to consciousness, something that makes demands on the entire being for balance. By being single, by either conscious or unconscious choice, you have cast yourself in a difficult and demanding role: the role of self-determination, self-growth and self-knowledge.

Because society still believes that something is wrong with you if you are single—especially if you are a woman—your task becomes one of seeing yourself clearly and rising above what "they" expect of you. The process of facing yourself, knowing yourself and being yourself has different rules from those you were taught in early childhood and adolescent culture. There is a weight and a substance to living alone because it makes demands on your ability to rely on yourself.

But that is also the beauty of being single: the terrible beauty of being single; the human beauty of loving and living in the moment and then letting the moment go; the divine beauty of coming into contact with higher, more creative planes because you have developed your inner resources.

Being single can bring out the artist in you. Demands on the self *are* to be made. Sacrifices *are* to be undertaken. Goals *are* to be defined. Perspectives *are* to be widened beyond the idea that marriage or coupling is the be-all and end-all.

Being single is the basic condition of every human being, a condition to celebrate and investigate with the courage and the conviction that we are who we are for a definite reason.

Who am *I?*

That is the question, the challenge and the opportunity of being single.

CHAPTER FIVE

The Twenties: Flying the Coop

Why is it that modern psychology, behaviorist at heart, has paid so much attention to the early years and left the young-to-middle adult years go virtually unnoticed? Why has modern psychology missed so many fundamental psychic rhythms that affect each and every one of us on a mass, universal level?

One of the most fundamental patterns of psychic development and ego maturation can be seen in the "mythical" seven-year cycles of a person's life. Although the timetable is not strict and rigid, there is a certain rhythm to the "normal" growth of a developing ego.

In the seventh year of life a child loses his first set of teeth and acquires his second. The fourteenth year sees completion of puberty. From fourteen to twenty-one, we experience the physical growth and emotional vulnerabilities of adolescence. At twenty-one there comes the urge to "fly the coop" and make one's own way in the world. At each stage, a fundamental change of *consciousness* takes place.

The changes from birth to age twenty-one are mainly physical. After twenty-one the changes that occur are more subtle and psychic in quality. Very often in the twenty-first year an individual feels the impulse to fly and explore, to set up a life of his or her own choosing. Not that this impulse is dormant until then—many feel it *before* the twenty-first year— but often the action of leaving home, of loosening ties, of cutting the umbilical cord once and for all does not take definite shape until then. In our present educational system twenty-one is a normal year of graduation from college.

At twenty-one years of age the inner psychic task becomes one of going out on one's own. A change of energy during the twenty-first year takes place as the young, still reactionary ego goes out to seek experience. To test raw capacities. To find a niche. To make something of the self in a public realm. To experiment. To say to the world in some way, "Hey, ready or not, here I come."

The inner impulse so powerful during the twenty-first year is to set *out,* to turn *out* into the social world, to set the self up in the real, everyday, make-a-living environment. Often there are periods of travel, changes of residence, a series of sexually oriented, thrill-seeking love affairs, an inner as well as outer search for a place to feel comfortable. The twenty-one to twenty-eight period is very much one of trial and error, in which the ego, the sense of "I am," seeks to establish a place in marriage, business or some form of worship of the sensual body. The young ego often seeks a freedom to define itself by its own impulses on its own terms. "Who am I?" the twenty-one to twenty-eight ego asks, expecting an answer from the environment.

The twenty-one- to twenty-eight-year-old ego looks on the *outside* for the meaning of life. From the ages of twenty-one to twenty-eight, one plays out the ideas and concepts of a child. There is a focus on the *personality,* which is essentially a reaction against or to the outer world. One seeks to do what is right, expected, adventurous or rebellious based on environmental inputs. There is not yet real freedom of choice because talents and capacities have not been refined by the school of hard knocks. One *reacts* to parents, to schooling, to strong sexual and sensual desires. The years from twenty-one to twenty-eight carry the formative forces in a very direct, yet largely unconscious way. The sense of self is very outer-directed, even if a person adopts the posture of the rebel or nonconformist.

The essential pattern of action is born out of what approaches the individual from without. The inner life very seldom has its own stamp because the freedom of choice—the conscious recognition of alternatives—has not yet been activated out of a clear and directed will. Both the rebel and the conformist play out unconscious ties to the experience of the past, in alternative styles.

In a sense, from twenty-one to twenty-eight you react to your lover. You seek to be in love for the *feeling* of being in love. You cultivate relationships as a substitute for the womb and the cocoon of your early years. You're often at the mercy of the outer world. You see yourself in and through the eyes of other people. Pleasure is visceral—hot, juicy and immediate. The here and now are everything. The before and after are too distant to visualize clearly. Although you have some intellectual urges to understand, codify and categorize your personal experience into units that your mind can comprehend rationally and empirically, even courses of advanced study come from the outside to impress themselves on the young ego. There is an implicit belief that the "real" world begins and ends on the material plane, that your real world can and should be measured on physical, social and environmental standards.

The result of this world concept is sometimes frightening, frustrating and difficult to bear. The world doesn't seem to live up to your expectations. As long as you depend on the outer, environmental realm for fulfillment, you are afraid of judgment, commitment and risk. You say, "I can love you, but only up to a certain point. I can't promise to love you forever. All I can speak for is the now, and now I want to take you to bed."

From twenty-one to twenty-eight, love is more a feeling than an action. There often is an intangible feeling that you will be rewarded when love does come along. Love will bring happiness, direction and purpose. When you are in love, you will be taken care of and you will care for your lover. Together two will grow as one, and that's the way it *should* be.

But love rarely happens that way, for singles *or* for married couples. The first idea of love is rarely the reality of love, so one of the first pieces of investigative work for any single person who still believes in the romantic concept of love at this stage is to look at those concepts which bombarded you in the past, especially during your high school and college days.

For example, write down in your personal inventory journal a few names of romantic relationships you had during the years from twenty-one to twenty-eight. Even if the relationship existed only as a fantasy in your head, write personal and specific answers to the following questions. Answer *all* the questions for *each name* you jot down.

1. What did you see love promise you through this person?

2. What did you have to give to this person? What *did* you give? Did you give all you could? If not, why not?

3. What were the conditions under which and the terms with which you gave love to each other? Did you know what you were doing?

4. What was the source of your love for this person?

> sexual?

> emotional?

> spiritual?

> other?

Explain each answer in your own words.

5. From twenty-one to twenty-eight, what did you think a love relationship *should* be with each of these people? Did you impose your *should* on him or her?

6. What was the *actual* give-and-take action with this person as compared to the *ideal?*

7. What kept you from reaching your ideal? Outer or inner circumstances? What role did you assume in each episode?

8. At twenty-one, did you see yourself single at twenty-eight? At thirty-five? At forty-two?

In the statistics gathered over three years in the singles class at Hunter, a representative sample of people from all over the United States, more than 85 percent did *not* see themselves single at twenty-eight when they were twenty-one. At twenty-eight, they did not see themselves flying solo at thirty-five. Yet all of them were.

Time seemed to fly by. The love that most thought would come to them by accident or by chance never did. Near misses didn't count. Many found themselves trapped in the waiting game, unaware that the lack of effort in the area of self-development and self-awareness had a negative, atrophying effect, much like neglecting to exercise a muscle or eating a diet without protein. At the outset of the program there was a widespread sense that being single was a temporary condition, a phase that one would simply be passing through. But the opposite proved to be true in real life.

Being single is *not temporary*. It is not a phase. It is not something that will take care of itself, nor will love just come along by chance.

Being single is *permanent* until a person begins to develop the capacities of positivity, risk and commitment to self. In fact, more and more evidence points to the probability that nothing occurs by chance. Every event, every happening, every condition has an internal chemistry.

If one is tentative in one's actions, tentative about goals, wants and alternatives, if one is afraid to speak out and take a chance in unfamiliar situations because of what other people may say, if one tends to hide and blame circumstances for depression or indifference, the time of being single will evolve into a chronic, terminal condition.

Why not assume that the outer circumstances of your life are a direct reflection of your inner attitudes and objectives?

That gives you a fighting chance to color the quality of your days and nights with your own starlight. Weak will leads to fear of flying. Ambiguous goals can leave you flying too low. Not wanting to can lead you to disaster. Aimless searching for the right man and the ideal woman leads to empty quests for the superfuck, cheap thrills or collecting assorted trinkets and baubles.

The psychic dynamics are difficult to bear at times because most of the activity occurs at a subliminal, unconscious plane. From twenty-one to twenty-eight, many singles play out ideas and concepts of love that they hardly know they have, especially in these days of electronic media. Those of us born about the time of World War II have been bombarded with tons of emotional, intellectual and material propaganda which our conscious minds filter out as a means of protection but which seep into the channels of the subconscious computer nonetheless.

For example, as a means of considering what your personal ideas of what love-should-be are, try writing down your ten favorite songs or record albums of all time. Your ten favorite movies. Ten favorite books. Songs, movies and books which have stayed with you all these years. Input from the outside which you have lived with and ingested so that they color the way you see the world around you.

After each one of these songs, movies or books, make a note of the basic concept. What was the point of view of the artist? What moved you? Why did this work have staying power? What was the *feeling* you digested so that it became a part of your repertoire?

For me, music was more influential than movies or books. Listening to the radio in the car or in my room, waiting for the Curly-Headed Kid in the Third Row (the title of the local DJ superstar) announce the number one record of 1955 was a big deal. I got myself a guitar, and music was in the air all the time. Pop music provided the foundation for my romantic dream castle.

I offer the following list of ten songs that left their mark on me from years zero to twenty-eight. These are my own personal peanut-butter songs, the ones that stuck to the roof of my mouth until they melted and became a part of me.

What are your own?

1. "Ghost Riders in the Sky"

I remember riding in our car with my father on a dark and rainy afternoon when I first heard this song on the radio. I must have been no more than five or six years old, and as I encountered that "Yippee ay oooooo, yippee ay ayyyyy" for the first time, I remember looking up and distinctly seeing ghost riders and the devil's herd "plowing through the ragged sky and up a cloudy draw."

At the time it seemed natural and obvious to me to assume that there was a connection between the heavens and the earth. I knew there was a definite relationship between what I did and what was recorded on a higher, although invisible, level. In my heart and in my gut, I knew that what I did counted and that someday there would be a kind of reckoning. Something was watching over me all the time. I would have to answer to some*thing*, some*body* at some *time*. At five or six years of age spirits were distinctly good or evil. There were people I liked and those I hated instantaneously. Something that came from them gave me the clue: a current, a color, a sensation.

One thing I didn't want. I didn't want to chase a herd of thundering, fiery-tongued steers across those endless skies forever and ever. There was something I had to *do*, somewhere I had to find, someplace I had to reach. That was why I was living. I was here for a reason, and I was scared.

The first thing that came to mind was to be a cowboy, and one day, frying pan in hand, I announced I was going off to Texas to help Bob Steele, Hoot Gibson and Tom Mix catch the rustlers.

I never did go off to Texas, but I also never lost the inner conviction that there was *something more* around me that I sensed but never could quite contact.

The invisible, the psychic, the electromagnetic, the clairvoyant, intuitive, imaginative, inspirational fields were very alive for me at five or six years old. There *were* ghost riders in the sky. Everything was *alive* and full of meaning.

Then I went to school.

2. "Auf Wiedersehen, Sweetheart"

> Although we're through,
> I'll wait for you.
> Auf wiedersehen, sweetheart.

In the second grade I fell in love with Vicki. Victoria Rogers. Who was in love with Bruce Fails, the dumbest kid in the class, the troublemaker. During the rest period I would lay my head in my arms on the desk and watch her long auburn hair fall over her shoulders. I'd bask in the beauty of her brown, oval eyes. I'd be entranced by her haunting, enticing smile.

Sometimes I'd pull her pigtails when she was playing with Bruce Fails. In the playground I would run after her and show her what a good ballplayer I was. But she never had eyes for me. She was in love with the dumbest kid in the class, and I was the smartest. What was wrong with her?

One day, again sitting listening to the car radio, I heard "Auf Wiedersehen, Sweetheart." My parents were shopping for groceries, and I allowed myself to cry because I knew that she would never love me the way I loved her. She would never love me the way she loved the dumbest kid in the class.

I couldn't understand her, but I could understand the pain in my heart. The pain of love started in the second grade, the first one ever.

I wonder where she is today. In a funny way, she's never, ever left me.

3. Theme song from *Moulin Rouge*
Remember José Ferrer as Toulouse-Lautrec, with the haunting song from *Moulin Rouge?* Paris in the 1890's....

I saw myself in that ugly little man who painted beautiful pictures. Who loved gorgeous, dancing women in cafés which sparkled with a life, lust and action that I had never known. *Paris.* Was there really such a place?

I promised myself that someday I would live in Paris. I would love in Paris. I would follow in Toulouse-Lautrec's stumpy little footsteps. I had the looks to fill the part. Also the heart.

4. "Where or When"

> It seems we stood and talked like this before.
> We looked at each other in the same way then,
> But I can't remember where or when.
>
> Some things that happen for the first time
> Seem to be happening again.
> And so it seems that we have met before
> And laughed before and loved before,
> But who knows where or when?

Have you ever been on vacation and felt that the new surroundings were familiar even though you had never been there before?

Have you ever felt an immediate magnetic attraction to someone and known there was some *inner* connection between the two of you? Is there, in fact, a path of destiny to walk where we encounter another person for a *reason?* What is this chemistry beyond words or rational explanation?

Before I ever cruised the streets of Manhattan, I knew I was home.

Before I ever climbed the ruins of Delphi, I knew there was unfinished business in that space.

A part of me reacted and came alive in these places. Something from a deep and distant past awakened, and although my present physical body made no distinctions, my inner psychic body sent out signal after signal.

The first time I saw Renee, I knew we would be lovers.

The first time I saw Jeanna, the same.

The first time I saw Deena, Kathryn, Lee, I knew.

Just as I know now that I have not yet met *the* one, my soulmate, to travel with forever. I don't know where or when, but I know I will. When I am ready. The inner alarm clock is going to go off someday when I am not looking for it. It has always happened that way. When I'm *not* looking.

Now to wait, trust, work and be all that I can be.

I still love the music of Rodgers and Hart, the Gershwins, Cole Porter, Harold Arlen, Johnny Mercer, Sammy Cahn, Lerner and Loewe—all those romantic, wonderful tunes from my lonely days in my attic room. I know all the words to all the songs from way back then.

5. "Heartbreak Hotel"

My mother was shocked and offended by the explosion of Elvis Presley on the scene in the mid-1950's. I was thirteen or fourteen at the time, and my attraction to his electric energy and blatant sexuality was a personal affront to her, as if she couldn't figure out where she had gone wrong.

She never did understand that beneath it all, Elvis sang:

> Now if your baby's left you
> And you've got a tale to tell
> Just take a walk down Lonely Street
> To Heartbreak Hotel.

Elvis was the first performer I loved whom my mother hated. Even to my adolescent consciousness, the choice was clear and obvious: Ike or Elvis. A style, a rhythm and a sense of self were at stake.

I couldn't remember D-Day—I was in the cradle and my father was in North Africa.

I had to go with what *I* knew, felt, liked.

6. "Chantilly Lace"

This was the first song that solidly focused my head and my heart between my legs. Or between the legs of every girl I could get the nerve up to talk to.

Chantilly lace and a pretty face
And a ponytail hanging down,
A wiggle in her walk,
And a giggle in her talk
Makes the world go round, round, round.

There ain't nothing in the world
Like a big-eyed girl,
Makes me act so funny
Makes me spend my money.
Makes me feel real loose,
Like a long-necked goose,
Like a girl.

Getting laid was everything. Sex was the jackpot. Females were cute little Kewpie dolls and were taught to be that way. To please a man. To run a house. To be pretty and frilly and stay on the surface of life.

I knew what the Big Bopper meant when he said, "OO-OOOOO, baby, you *know* what I like." Everybody did.

In the car. On the beach. In the fraternity house. Anywhere, anytime, anyhow. Leave 'em laughing when you go.

Leonard Cohen once had a character in a novel say, "I stopped fucking faces when I was fifteen." I didn't. And I'm sure neither did the Big Bopper. Right up to the end. I felt bad when he died. I thought he had it *all*.

7. "Scotch and Soda"

By the time I had reached my twenty-first year I had learned that making my own music was a way to get to the girls without the girls getting to me. Then, one night in February, I found Renee, who looked like Audrey Hepburn in *Breakfast at Tiffany's*. I took her back to the fraternity house and lit a fire. I played "Scotch and Soda" on the guitar five times, and we were in love with each other for the whole spring semester. We watched flowers bloom and made love in the grass under warm and starry skies.

In March I discovered she was an heiress to a multimillion-dollar fast food chain in Buffalo, New York. Her mother didn't like my talking to her about Albert Camus, Dostoevsky and Norman O. Brown. Her mother had "class." In June her mother gave her the choice of me-or-the-family. Renee told me she loved me and would always love me, but she couldn't handle the pain or the tension at home. She didn't want me anymore.

When she left to marry her grammar-school Romeo, I played "Scotch and Soda" for six years and never felt anything for anybody. There were blues in the night.

I saw San Francisco, Los Angeles, Greece, London, and I passed through Paris in two days.

8. "Just Like a Woman"

I was in my twenty-first year when November 22, 1963, in Dallas changed everything. Everyone in my generation heard Bob Dylan, Joan Baez and the voices in the South. Dylan made me cry, feel, think, fight. Dylan opened the doors of

Berkeley to me, and I cried in rage when I witnessed the
Oakland police smash the peace marchers on that warm,
lovely day at the Oakland-Berkeley city line. The Hell's
Angels "broke" the police line and crashed the skulls of the
marchers who had sat down en masse. Blood was everywhere,
and people sang the songs of Dylan for strength and comfort.

Everywhere I went I would play "Just Like a Woman."
Everyone knew the words. Everyone knew where the words
came from. In Berkeley and in the West Village in the 1960's
it was we against them. I threw up when I saw the main event
in Chicago in 1968, yet Dylan was always there as conscience,
as inspiration, as voice of humanity and reason.

I stayed with a woman for three years on and off. Our best
scenes were at airports, the comings and the goings. Near the
end I would think about somebody else when making love to
her. I chose to believe that the real reason for our breakup
was that she had LA in her blood and I had New York in
mine.

> When we meet again and are introduced as friends
> Please don't let on that you knew me when
> I was hungry and it was your world.

I asked her to marry me only when I knew it was too late—
when she had made a big hit in Hollywood and when I
wanted to ride in on her coattails.

She laughed and said *no*. On the radio Dylan was singing
about going nowhere. I felt something was lost when I hopped
the next plane, but I always thought I'd see her again.

9."You've Got to Hide Your Love Away"
Where Dylan was political and romantic, the Beatles were
psychedelic and mind-blowing. Dylan hit me in the gut, but
the Beatles hit me in the head. *Sgt. Pepper* and *Abbey Road,*
side two, made me *see* and *think* differently. But I would still
go back, in the still of night, to the dire need for love—the

need for a woman to complete my life and supply the missing half.

> How could she say to me, "Love will find a way?"
> Gather round, all you clowns, let me hear you say
> Hey, you've got to hide your love away.

All the pieces would not fit. Something I was doing was wrong. A short circuit somewhere. The Beatles told me to look in my own head on the way to my own heart.
Whom could I turn to? *To myself.*
Isn't that what the Beatles really said?

10. "Suzanne"
Dylan turned troubadour. The Beatles retreated to the Maharishi and big money, but Leonard Cohen lived with muses in Hydra and wrote poems that stood up without music. "Suzanne" had a quality of mystery and magic that I recognized from some place in my cosmic past, and I began to see more of what was *there* rather than what I *wanted* to be there.

> You know that she's half crazy
> But that's why you want to be there
> And she feeds you tea and oranges
> That come all the way from China.
>
> And you want to travel with her
> You want to travel blind
> And you know that you will trust her
> Because she's touched your perfect body
> With her mind.

Cohen added the spiritual dimension, the angst of past choices intruding on the present, fashioned in and acted out of the subconscious. With Cohen's "Bird on the Wire," "Famous Blue Raincoat" and "So Long, Marianne" came the recognition and the wonder of self-determination.

Cohen whispered:

> I met a man who lost his mind
> In some lost place I had to find.
> "Follow me," the wise man said,
> But he walked behind.

Something happened to me at twenty-eight.

During the years from twenty-one to twenty-eight, there is not that much pressure about being single. Especially in our society where educational opportunities are more and more widespread and consciousness about male-female roles is being "raised," there is a growing feeling that these years are designed to be experimental. Both men and women are to test the job market, set up living facilities according to individual tastea and "have fun" with relationships which may or may not last forever.

In the twenties the developing ego can afford to experiment with love, sex and travel. There is a resiliency and an exuberance which allow one to rebound after hurts and disappointments because you are *supposed* to play the field and enjoy your freedom. There is often a hit-or-miss quality about these years, and because time is a luxury, you can fall into and out of love with the sense that one day everything will just fall into place. By itself. Because love, happiness and fulfillment are a birthright. Something you are to have just because you are who you are. Nothing to worry about. Whatever will be will be.

But sometime in the twenty-eighth or twenty-ninth year something happens to change the entire picture. In the circumstantial environment there will often be a romantic, emotional crisis. A relationship will be thrown into conflict by one of the two partners. A career will come to a turning point.

Everything that seemed arbitrary and haphazard, a function of chance, comes into a different perspective. You begin to face your fantasies and realize that in a very strange way, you have been ultimately responsible for yourself.

Nobody is doing *it* to you. The time for experimentation is over. It's time to get serious and develop some inner resources. The external world proves itself to be vicious, expedient, self-serving and somewhat absurd. There is another, more elusive, more dangerous and more provocative realm—the area within yourself.

That inner life is now ready to extend toward more invisible, intangible, spiritual realms of principled behavior or it will be ensnared more deeply in adolescent dreams, fears and fantasies. This is not a very pleasant time as your ideas and deeds start to rebound with an uncommon force. The wrestling match is with the angel within, who demands the best and who offers peace of mind, purpose and guidance as a reward. Only by saying Yes! to the inner potentials can you get off the ground and fly solo. No more safety catches, no more protective blankets. Go it alone, or forever be a prisoner.

The following story illustrates a pattern of action that happens to many people in the late twenties. An intense relationship is brought into a new light; there is a flight toward fantasy; the fantasy proves to be an illusion. You are then stripped clean, forced to discipline yourself and make a reevaluation of what you want, need and desire.

In the spring of his twenty-eighth year, he was living with a woman. The fashion of the times fostered a try-it-before-you-buy-it attitude in both of them. Neither of them wanted to think about forever after, preferring to believe that fate had brought them together and would separate them when the time was right. She had a two-year-old son. She was nineteen.

After a month of laughter, smoke and sex she found herself

pregnant despite the birth control pills. Three months later she had an abortion. It took three hospital trips plus one emergency ambulance ride to kill the fetus. The abortion killed the relationship. He woke up one morning with a calling to flee to Europe.

On the plane to London he witnessed the sunrise in the sky. Driving over the mountains of Yugoslavia, he witnessed the sunrise over a misty valley. On the boat from Brindisi to Patras, he witnessed the sunrise over the Mediterranean. He was penniless, loveless, homeless, yet awake at dawn on three different airplanes.

In Greece he lost his most precious gift: language. Words taken away, all he had left was a longing, a desperate need to be involved. At the airport in Athens he was charged $40 for overweight luggage. He had to pay or stay. He paid.

In Munich, *Oktoberfest.* No rooms. Beer-filled halls with sloppy bourgeois singing. Carnival. For him, Germany was still Hitler.

A play at the Kammerspiele. An actress onstage. Intelligent, graceful, spiritual. A nude scene where her body looked like the statue of a Greek goddess. Backstage, after the show, he arranged a rendezvous. His dream come true, he made his move.

She took him to a café away from the carnival. Artists, writers, composers, dancers. Mellow jazz. Tables with candles and blue-checkered cloths. She spoke to him in English. They held hands, danced, whispered. At 4 A.M. they were the last couple in the café. She didn't want the night to end. She was everything he had ever dreamed about. She was his new dawn.

Outside she fell silent, walked slowly. Rain glistened in the streets. He asked her to come with him, first to London, then to New York. She stopped in front of a house with closed shutters. He expected to be invited in.

"There's somebody upstairs," she said. "I wish there wasn't, but there is."

He turned away. Crushed. His dream come true vanished in

the night. He left in the morning. High fever in Berlin. Back to London. A message from the nineteen-year-old. When would he be back home?

Where to go? Which way to turn? Where to find *the* answer? "Back home," an aborted affair. Munich, a love pledged to another.

A moment of truth. Banging up against a fantasy face to face. Falling in love with an image, an actress on a stage acting out a play about real life, an illusion with no substance. Somehow everything he had ever wanted, conditioned by the books, movies and songs he had grown up with, was nothing.

Going back meant retreat. Moving ahead meant letting go of ideals. He played it safe. He went back to the States. After two more nights together he never saw the nineteen-year-old again.

The twenty-eighth and twenty-ninth years offer a crisis of self-determination. No longer can the single hero and heroine be as optimistic or as casual as they once were. A reckoning is in store—a self-evaluation which will reinforce old patterns or initiate new ones. Especially for women, the prospect of having a family life grows dimmer, and alternatives must be sought to fill the requirements of a meaningful life. Thoughts about yourself must change consciously and painfully, or else war is declared on the self. Twenty-eight and twenty-nine offer truce or war, and the battleground is within.

In the twenty-eighth and twenty-ninth years, life circumstances shake up old ideas of what is real, true and valuable. That inner turmoil, reflected in outer events, is part of a cosmic scheme to test the individual's ability to define and refine his inner, innate, often dormant talents. Sex doesn't seem to matter. Everyone, man and woman, passes through this stage consciously or unconsciously. In a paradoxical way, those who struggle with their angel during this period have the best chance of realizing themselves and making peace with their spiritual dimension.

The resolution of this stage of life determines the quality of life for the next seven years. The test seems to be to find yourself under internal pressure, to find yourself as an individual regardless of social customs and demands and to develop inner resources by confronting yourself honestly and directly time and time again.

The questions at twenty-eight are often the same as those at twenty-one.

Who are you?

What do you really want?

Where are you going?

What are you working for?

The questions are similar, but one octave higher. The same questions carry a greater weight. More seems to be at stake. Ideas need to be acted on rather than thought about. Actions seem to have consequences on planes you did not notice earlier on. What you *are* can be seen by what you *do*. There is definitely a connection between the inner and outer life, and for most people, the inner life of personal resources has been sadly neglected.

We have been taught, as a society, to value materialistic things and to ignore the intangible resources within. We have been seduced by the easy life and trapped within the body, but we have a safety valve implanted deep within that makes itself known in the late twenties.

At that time we will be asked to make a commitment, first to ourselves, then to a community and then to a set of principles that go beyond the immediate, the expedient and the sensual. We are asked to control our appetites and make demands on ourselves as individuals. We have the chance to be all that we could be or to repeat old patterns.

Commitment, control, conscious effort to understand one's own self-chemistry—that's what happened to many people with great intensity in the late twenties.

Did it happen to you? What did you do about it?

CHAPTER SIX

The Thirties: Saturn Returns

During the late 1960's, for a whole generation of post-World War II, post-Kennedy, Vietnam-disillusioned individuals, thirty years of age marked a distinct, definite and dramatic turning point. Thirty years old was the sellout age, when dreams, ideals and humanitarian pursuits went out the window into corporate structures and suburban shades of gray, green and pastel. Thirty was the dividing line—another demarkation between us and them, yet suddenly, irrevocably, without doing anything, we became one of *them*.

There was no doubt about it. At twenty-eight, at twenty-nine and into the thirtieth year, a severe change of energy took place. In the twenty-eighth year something happened inside. In the twenty-ninth year that inward landscape became troubled, tested and thrown topsy-turvy. In the thirtieth year we knew it was time to get serious and come to terms with the individual and collective soul. We had to square ourselves with ourselves *first*.

This period of time, the twenty-eighth, twenty-ninth and thirtieth years, is called the Saturn Return period because it is a time of inner confrontation with the self and a time of reevaluation of ideas, beliefs, concepts and actions. During this period some event, circumstance or relationship will intensify to the boiling point and throw an individual back on his own resources in such a way that has never happened before.

Because modern psychological theories have largely ignored this intense, inward period of reevaluation, we have to look to other areas for "explanations." Although it is not my wish to convince anyone of the truth or falsity of astrology, this metascience does point to some interesting celestial energy patterns that occur to *everybody* during his twenty-eighth, twenty-ninth and thirtieth years. Since an inward change is felt consciously by many individuals as a shift in *energies,* I would simply like to present the astronomical facts and the corresponding psychological effects for the consideration of the reader.

Mathematically Uranus takes seven years to pass through one sign of the zodiac, which is one cosmic connection to the seven-year cycles already suggested. According to tradition, Uranus is the planet of change, originality, eccentricity, electrical energy and unexpected events. In the twenty-eighth year, therefore, a person is just beginning the fifth Uranian cycle. At the same time other potent configurations in the solar system are at work.

When a person reaches the age of twenty-eight, the progressed moon reaches the same position it held at the moment of his or her birth. The moon has made a transit through every sign in the zodiac and thus has made a conjunction with every planet in the natal horoscope. In short, by the time you have reached your twenty-eighth year, you have had a "once around" with your moon energies and have now had experience in every "house" of your life. At this point either you progress consciously through an active choice or you repeat the patterns of the first twenty-eight years.

The planet Neptune takes fourteen years to travel through one sign of the zodiac, so at the twenty-eighth year, it forms a sextile to its natal position—meaning that it is 60 degrees away from where it was at the moment of birth. This sextile inspires an urge to creativity, a move to spirituality, a questioning of the meaning, purpose and direction of life. The Neptunian energies are psychic and intuitive, inner and creative, and there is a desire to dig deeper into the self when this event occurs in the twenty-eighth year.

Finally and most important, Saturn takes twenty-nine and a half years to make one complete revolution in its orbit. At twenty-nine and a half, Saturn is in the same position as it was at birth. Saturn is often called the Great Malefic because it brings tests, trials and limitations, as well as a need for self-discipline and self-determination. Saturn is the greatest "teacher" of all the planet energies, and when it "focuses" its energies on any given individual—as it does on all people in the twenty-ninth year of life—a serious time of self-questioning and self-understanding comes along.

If you agree that the moon forces affect the earth's tides and the moods of individuals, you must entertain the possibility of other cosmic energies' also affecting individuals in an unconscious way. All celestial bodies have electromagnetic forces contained within them which affect the earth's field in a daily, universal way. Too often we are blind to these energy fields that surround and influence us.

But these esoteric, astrological, astronomical facts become even more intriguing and thought-provoking when psychological equivalents are spelled out and specified in more here-and-now detail. Think back over your own experiences, and recall the times, places and situations of your twenty-eighth, twenty-ninth and thirtieth years. What happened to you? What changed? Did you have a conscious handle on yourself and those events at that time?

If you are like many other singles who have gone through

the Saturn Return, the following thoughts and feelings might have passed through you at that magic age:

1. My concept of love has undergone a drastic change. I thought love would simply come to me, but now I know I have to work for it, giving something of myself without expectation of specific reward. I feel I need to extend myself to others, but I cannot seem to fit all the pieces together with myself, much less with another human being. Being single is not temporary but permanent until I can choose and act on a different pattern of life from the one I have had up to this point. Everything I have done now seems superficial and unconscious.

2. The thrill of love is gone—if not vanished, certainly transformed. The hot spots, the getting high, the getting laid, the erotic dances are held for someone special and more permanent. Emotional investments are made with more care and caution. I can't afford to fuck around anymore. All artificial means of getting off, getting high or getting it on are questioned, then seen through as illusory. The more I look on the outside for fulfillment, the farther I am away from that fulfillment.

3. At twenty-eight I feel that drastic turn inward, drastic because I feel overpoweringly that I have done nothing, I am going nowhere in my present course, and everything that seemed *everything* now seems like nothing. At twenty-one I asked the questions "Who am I?" and "Where am I going?" in my head, but now those questions come from the heart and gut. There is a different weight, a higher octave at stake. My inner life has been moved up a notch, and that which I could afford to ignore because of my youth now stares me in the face. I have to come to terms with myself. My personality—my reaction to the outer world—has been my underlying concern, but now my individuality is calling me forward. All crutches must be thrown away so I can heal myself and walk. The bottom line is who I am by myself, with myself, for myself.

Nobody can do it for me. I am truly my own person. God damn it, why have I wasted so much *time?*

4. At twenty-eight and twenty-nine a marriage, coupling or partnership was severely tested or fell apart. Again, something happened that made me feel I had been blind and insincere. I played at being in love and never gave anything from the deepest level. At twenty-eight and twenty-nine, I felt a compulsion from within to break this tie in order to find myself and then to give to another person from a conscious perspective rather than from a childish, unconscious urge. I fell madly in love in my twenties, and now that love seems a little mad. I am not happy with my love partner because I am not happy with myself. I need my own space, my own time and the chance to be all that I want to be. To do that, I have to be alone, at least for a while.

5. The emotional upheaval brings the gnawing sensation that I have been wasting my time in *tentative* actions. I have been going through the motions and have not taken any risks. I have not committed myself to anything that is real in a psychic way. My inner life has been a vacuum, filled by winds that blew in from unknown regions. Now I have to ventilate my system. I need to let out all the foul, rotting smells that I have stored in my closet like cherished toys since childhood. I need to look at those skeletons in the light—or else get hung in the closet with them.

6. The change in the inner quality of my life at twenty-eight, at twenty-nine and into my thirtieth year has much to do with my place in the universe. Once the question of "Where am I going?" referred to a job, a profession, a lover or a family—making a living on strictly an earth plane—but now this question begins to have a cosmic, spiritual, universal dimension. At twenty-eight and twenty-nine I start to wonder about the grand designs of the universe and question why I was born. I seek to make a link to a realm beyond the environmental and to see myself as a spiritual being. I begin to believe that I existed *before* my present body in a different

condition. *I am not my body.* There is something inside me that is not physical, not material and not measurable by any rational, scientific, computerized standard. There is something in me that makes me *me,* and to find and use that *me* are my task.

Somehow I have computed my own singleness at this stage of my life for a reason that I knew nothing about, but that is coming to light only now. I need to make a link with something greater than myself by finding myself through discrimination, choice and action. It begins to dawn on me that it is *right* that I am single; before I can or should couple, I have to be at home with myself. Dues must be paid; the shortcuts I took all those years are rebounding against me now. I know that I don't know what I thought I knew. Now it seems I know nothing; only surfaces, only impressions, only tidbits of information. I was born to fly, and now I am lame and limping. Was Icarus real?

7. I've become painfully aware that I've been given very special, individualized gifts which I have not taken advantage of—especially in the areas of creativity, composition and regeneration. I have found and documented everything that was wrong with the world order. Now it seems it is my destiny to create something positive out of the negative. There is not enough time to stall and make believe that everything will work out fine. What I do to myself and to others does matter.

Some higher plateau is waiting for me. Only my work on myself can elevate me to that higher ground. Before, my basic idea of life was to offend, defend or suspend my feelings. Now the idea is to extend them. More and more I find it necessary to change the basic attitude of my life from What can I get from you? to What can I do for you? I barely begin to see that I have to *create* to stay alive. No matter what I do for money, comfort or pleasure, there is another part of me which needs to be nourished, exercised and refined—my creative soul.

8. Despite my formal education, I've come to realize how deficient I've been in my thinking, feeling and willing. My

thoughts have been generated by outside stimuli. My feelings and moods swing like pendulums in some mysterious grandfather's clock. My will is almost nonexistent. I start and stop, start and stop, and cannot seem to bring any idea into being.

9. I am solely responsible for the *quality* of my life. I have lived mainly in my head, confined by my intellect and my fantasies, for many years. I have not yet tapped my deepest capacities, which reside far beyond my intellect. My reason can serve to unlock gut feelings and inner depths and is to be used only as a tool and an instrument for penetration into the psychic and spiritual world. Somehow I come to realize the existence of some master plan. My task becomes one of alignment and adjustment to both the social and the invisible forces of universal law. My tiny, personal pain becomes diminished compared to the pattern of action of the invisible currents and forces. Suddenly not only do I take myself more seriously, but I also look at Jesus, Buddha, Copernicus, Kant, Jung, Einstein, Rudolf Steiner and the metaphysicians more earnestly. The notion of reincarnation as a process of metamorphosis—the same being changing forms constantly—becomes more real as I travel to different parts of the earth and have queasy sensations that *I have been here before.* Finding my home and locating a space where I can live comfortably become an inner need, a driving force, an energy that *makes* me look within.

10. Fantasies have kept me fixated, playing out the same scenario time and time again. My love affairs have repeatedly gone stale, and my work seems routine and mechanical because I have never gone as far as I can go. The boy wonder I was at twenty-three is now an average Joe when seen in relation to others in the marketplace. My major task is now to cut away the excess emotional freight and somehow to get clear.

I need to distinguish between the essential and the nonessential and truly to understand that material *things* are not the answer. Sex is not the answer. Armpits that smell like flowers are not the answer. Alcohol is not the answer. Marijuana depletes the will, and hard drugs are straight poison to the spirit. Tobacco smoke is pollution of the soul. I can choose the kind of person I want to be, but first I have to live with myself as friend, partner and lover. I am *important* because of my body, soul and spirit. I can define myself by what I do for other people. My own pleasures are fleeting, but a moment of love, giving and sharing will echo in my heart forever.

How can I create the conditions of love?

Such are the thoughts and feelings of many single people during the years of the Saturn Return—sometimes mashed, sometimes mingled, sometimes depressing or elating, always with a weight and a color that cannot be ignored. From twenty-one to twenty-eight they experimented and strode boldly out into the world for recognition, thrills and fortune, shunning all direct supervision as archaic, square and limiting. They tried everything once and made no value judgments without direct experience.

But the heavy changes at twenty-eight make them see a little differently. No longer do they have to drink a whole bottle of milk to know it is sour. They can pick up signals at the moment of delivery rather than three hours later. Here they consciously begin the apprenticeship stage, which will last for seven years. They will be asked to practice what they preach as business opportunities come more readily and artistic pursuits become more demanding. It is almost as if some higher force, omniscient and intuitive, kept asking during these years from twenty-eight to thirty-five: What do you really want? What are you doing to get it? Are you cleaning up your act?

These are the difficult dues-paying years, and most people cannot muster up enough will to perfect their craft. Life is too hard. Recreational sex is too available. Patience is a virtue of the past. Perseverance is not worth the effort. They'd rather sit back and watch a football game on television than go out and play on the field themselves. They find themselves leveling off, but so what? Doesn't it happen to everybody?

Yet, if a person begins to take his inner life seriously and consciously develops that one talent which is death to hide, the years from twenty-eight to thirty-five take on a completely different tone. If an individual commits himself or herself to the inner light and to the voice within, a certain strength, confidence and creative rejuvenation emerge. The ability to bring an abstract idea into the material plane begins to mature. More and more opportunities to give of the self appear. As if by magic, as one starts to work on oneself *first* with a day-to-day dedication to a specific goal carved out of conscious choice, he or she begins to feel some inner need to go public—to take craft, talent and ideas into the public domain. As one works on oneself, he or she is given the chance to affect others with the quality of his inner being. The commodity he has to sell becomes himself—but in a wholesome and creative way. Because he cares enough to sign his work, he is no longer anonymous. He takes pride in what he does, in how he lives and in how he deals with people. The style of his actions becomes as important as the content.

In the seven-year cycle from twenty-eight to thirty-five, many single people go through a psychic change. New feelings and thoughts replace the values, concerns and ideals of youth. Specific, *practical* goals replace arbitrary wanderings to perfumed beds and exotic lands. A spiritual self-evaluation replaces abstract intellectual pursuits for monetary, professional or knowledge-for-knowledge's sake rewards. "How can you be all that you can be?" is a question taken out of the realm of theoretical and thrown back into practical here and now. You want to write down, objectify and understand repeated patterns which have served only to separate you from your inner, creative, spiritual self. You want to gain an inside track on the *reasons* for your actions. You want to spot the people, places and situations which limit and frustrate you.

This seven-year period of self-questioning, self-testing and self-determination will end with either great freedom or severe depression. Either you become truly self-sufficient by taking personal inventory after personal inventory, or you repeat the past. This taking stock of yourself does not have to be carried out with a sense of drudgery or angst. You are not putting your merchandise on the shelves in a close-out sale!

By making demands on your creative talents, by practicing a course of ego development and by committing yourself to the *action* that your inner life creates the quality of the outer life, you come to realize your higher self. The underlying test of all the events in the years between twenty-eight and thirty-five lies in making discriminations, judgments and choices about who you are, what you want and where you are going. Since greatest obstacles are still within, look for actions which are practical but spiritual at the same time. Look at the past to mold the future.

The Saturn Return period is filled with trauma, separation, depression, retreat and self-defeat. If a person does not know that these tests are coming as a matter of course in normal ego development, these years can be a tremendous shock to the soul. Yet single people actually have an advantage during these years in that they do not have to pull the freight of a mate or small children. Being single during the Saturn Return is a tremendous opportunity for growth, awareness and future determination. By being alone, truly *alone,* during these years, any individual can finally cut the umbilical cord of limited concepts and find his or her own center. Once centered and in balance, the Wheel of Fortune will more toward its destiny. The most comforting aspect of this period is that it happens to *everybody.*

As Hemingway reminds us in *The Sun Also Rises,* the bill always comes. Saturn has been interpreted as the cosmic bill collector, knocking on the door every twenty-nine and a half years. The debts that are to be paid are essentially debts to the self and the creative soul. As in "real," commercial enterprises, interest builds against you as the years accumulate. The loan you took from your parents, your education and your society years ago come back at you and demand a balancing of accounts.

Cutting off the excess is the ultimate task of the artist, poet or businessman. Recognizing and letting go of negative habits are the crosses we bear. Making choices out of a confident, positive field of vision becomes the opportunity. Love becomes an action, a commitment and a partnership now or—or it probably never will at all.

Getting together with another human being for a long-term, loving relationship does become more difficult as the years go by *if* an individual does not learn how to live comfortably with himself or herself. Living comfortably with yourself *always* demands a reevaluation of goals, standards, ideals and principles. If you lose contact with the higher self by tuning out of of the higher octave, be prepared for isolation and despair.

It's that simple.

The way out of loneliness, rejection and despair is to tune into your creative, psychic self. These capacities exist in *everyone*. All the exercises suggested in this book to this point are *specific, practical* ways of tuning into the creative channels. By answering the questions already suggested in this book in your own words in your own journal, you can write a book of your own. Without even trying to be creative, by reading this book and using it, you can start your own turn inward and upward. Where you go from there will depend on the effort you make.

Talent is *never* a question. Courage, trust and perseverance are the keys to all personal, social and psychological success as a single person. Although the cosmic timetable provides a "ripe" time to begin a creative turn inward during the Saturn Return years, it is never too late to start. It is only a matter of taking a few minutes for yourself during the evening to prepare the soil for the seed of creativity to take root and bloom. Do not expect instant magic from your exercises. The creative, spiritual well runs deep and dark. You will have to pull your own weight and find your own checks and balances. A teacher can provide you with the first tasks, but soon your task will be to determine your own task.

To cultivate your own soul is to develop the faculties of thinking, feeling and willing. As a means of preparing your own soil, I offer these six basic exercises as they are suggested by Rudolf Steiner in *The Knowledge of Higher Worlds and Its Attainment.*

1. Thought Concentration

How well do you *think?*

Before you leap to conclusions, try this little experiment. Choose a simple object, like a piece of chalk or a safety pin. Concentrate your thoughts on the object for five minutes. The task is not to allow any other thoughts to enter your field of consciousness. Keep focusing on the object and the concept behind the form. How did it come into being? At what point in history did it make its first appearance? How did it get to be the shape it is *now?*

If you are like the majority of people, your thoughts will stray away in fewer than five minutes. You will find yourself wandering into judgment, criticism or a feeling of not being able to do this *stupid* exercise! This shows only how out of control our thinking normally is. Thinking is usually based on sense impressions coming into the brain from the outside, and only rarely is thought generated from within.

The most intriguing aspect to this exercise is the correlation between outer-generated thinking and the sense of being out of control. If you are not able to control your thinking and the source of your own thought, you are unable to control the quality of your life.

Yet thinking can be the link to the spiritual world and the

foundation for self-confidence, self-acceptance and self-worth. Thinking can be raised above the personal sets of craving and desire to the plateau of principle, morality and universal law. As thinking becomes attuned to the concept level, it becomes the source of action rather than reaction. You can motivate yourself by your thoughts rather than depend on circumstance, chance or the whims of others.

This exercise of thought concentration—taking a simple object and focussing on the concept behind the form—has a gestation period of at least thirty days—thirty straight days. If you start and stop after two or three days, the rules state that you go back to square one. Every time you stop, for whatever reason, you pull out the sprout you have planted. Because you are training an inner dimension not usually exercised in school or business in a conscious way, you cannot really judge these exercises intellectually. There is no way of telling what the effects will be before you actually complete the process.

One of the most startling results of this exercise is that your dreams will become more alive and memorable. By consciously concentrating your thoughts on an object *as an exercise,* your unconscious faculties will open up. The rejuvenating processes that occur during sleep become accessible to conscious investigation. You will open an inside track to yourself as you commit this exercise to your *daily* routine.

2. Control of Action

Have you ever tried to perform the same action at the *exact* same time every day? Something simple but nonmonumental like winding your watch at 7:32 A.M. or changing your keys from one pocket to another at 3:13 P.M.? Something that you can do anywhere and that depends on no one but yourself for completion?

This is the second phase of preparing your inner soil, and you will add it to the thought concentration exercise when you

have practiced the first exercise for thirty straight days. The
second is an exercise in pure will because the action has no
direct consequence in your daily affairs. Nothing motivates
you to wind your watch at 7:32 A.M. each day but the idea of
exercising your will. The timing has to be *exact*. Doing it at
7:25 or 7:47 is not good enough. Precision is of the utmost
importance here. Choose a time carefully so that you will
always be awake and active, and make your gesture in-
conspicuous and silent.

One woman, having practiced the control of thought for
thirty days, thought for a while before choosing her gesture
for the control of action. She decided simply to fold her
hands, with her fingers intertwined, over her solar plexus,
almost as if in silent, momentary prayer. The gesture of
uniting her two hands at the exact same time every day
seemed to unify her and remind her of her higher octave.

A wonderful event started to happen to her about a week
into this exercise. Because she was devoted to the idea of
developing her will, an inner alarm clock buzzed inside her a
few minutes before the moment she had chosen. By making
conscious choices and inputs, she awakened a subconscious,
subliminal force in her soul which seemed to work with her.
This inner alarm clock is similar to the one which will wake
you if you decide to wake at a certain time in the morning.
When you give yourself a conscious directive, the subconscious responds with information that can guide and direct
you. When you start to feel this inner buzz a few minutes
before the exact time of your action, you have another signal
that the voice within is alive and well and living in your soul.

As with all the exercises in this book, success is measured
by consistent effort rather than by immediate tangible results.
Of course, you will notice a growth in strength, confidence
and ability to give of yourself to other people, but be assured
that even greater results are taking place in unconscious
regions. You are only preparing the soil. The fruit of your
efforts is still some time away.

The control of action exercise also has a gestation period of at least thirty straight days. Exercises one and two should be practiced together until they become part of your bloodstream. *Then* move on to exercise three.

3. The Refinement of Feeling

Whereas you can select certain times to perform exercises one and two, the refinement of feeling exercise can be practiced at any time, in any place, in any situation. The task of this exercise is to be aware when you are feeling anything emotionally—hate, fear, love, anger, indifference—and to ask yourself: *"What message is this feeling bringing to me?"*

Assume that feelings are messengers carrying lessons to learn which are essential to your growth and emotional health. *In the moment,* try to catch the reason that feelings are being aroused in you. *In the moment,* remember to see yourself from a higher perspective. *In the moment,* remember not to forget what you are doing.

Those who practice this exercise report an interesting phenomenon. Instead of losing spontaneity, they become more able to feel and express their feelings. By becoming attuned to the sense that feelings are messages from the voice within, a person becomes more able to act upon what he feels rather than repress those feelings.

A person becomes able to be *in* and *above* the immediate event at the same time. So instead of wasting time, energy and goodwill in rebuking yourself about what you should have said three hours or five days ago, or what you will tell your lover the next time he or she pulls an inconsiderate act, this exercise enables you to think on your feet and say what you mean.

This exercise leads to a directness and an economy of action that lift you above the "ordinary" level of fear, doubt and insecurity while you feel something deeply from the solar plexus. Instead of being paralyzed by feelings, you become better able to act on them at the moment you have them.

Since you do not know when you will have an inner feeling during the course of the day, you must be ready *all the time*. This is where your experience in the thought concentration and control of action exercises become important building blocks to action and confidence. If you skip the first two exercises, chances are that you will not be able to identify, much less remember, the question of exercise three. There is a real sense of progressive difficulty to these exercises, so that one builds on the last. There is a step-by-step pattern of action to inner ego development just as there is a natural process for a seed to bear fruit. There are no shortcuts.

4. Positivity

When you feel comfortable with the first three exercises, it is time to add the fourth, which is called positivity. This exercise involves finding the positive even in negative situations. The task is to change the negative to the positive by *understanding* that every event, person and situation you face can bring you information about yourself and your higher octave. Everything that happens has an internal chemistry, and instead of dissipating yourself in rebukes or self-defensiveness, you engage yourself with the inner action of every event.

The exercise can change your entire attitude about yourself, your position in life and your reason for being. As you look for the positive, you tend to find it in places that will surprise and astonish you.

One day, while stuck in a line at a bank, I reminded myself to change the negative to the positive, and I wrote down this little poem on the back of a deposit slip:

"There is a golden rule,"
said the hermit
to the fool waiting
on line, talking to himself
about the evils of banking
and impersonal deals for money.

"Before you can see
and hear with your heart,
you must rid yourself
of all impatience.

"Nothing of the higher realms
will be revealed to you
until you learn to wait
in silence,
to understand that cosmic trials
come in the most mundane of costumes.

"Write a poem.
Say a prayer.
Search your soul.
Observe your fellow creatures
as if this were your last
five minutes
on the face of the earth.

"What you do on line
right here and now
is your last dance
before death."

5. Tolerance

Exercise five grows out of the ability to wait on line without
annoyance. Added to the first four, it builds a certain attitude

toward the obstacles of life. Every living human being can count on roadblocks in every stage of life, but each person is also capable of seeing these roadblocks as opportunities for growth rather than as detours from tasks.

The exercise of tolerance builds power as it points up the possibility of accepting what exists as a means of understanding and growth. Instead of criticizing or rushing to judgment, banish your inherited skepticism and reticence. When you find the positive and listen without criticism, almost every human interaction can inspire you to see the joy of being. Tolerance of others builds a tolerance and a love for the self, and nothing is more attractive or magnetic than a person who accepts himself and others for what they are at the moment.

But the practice of tolerance goes farther. To just tolerate another person is silently to give him the feeling that you are putting up with his crazy foibles. There is nothing more annoying than to be tolerated. The spirit of this exercise has a more active aspect. Tolerance implies an extension of yourself toward another person. You send a current out rather than merely hold back critical thoughts.

The difference is very subtle but noticeable to others. Passive tolerance gives you a sense of knowing it all and doing the other person a favor for being here. Active tolerance means that you are inviting another into your orbit to share an experience. As always, the *quality* of your action counts for the success or failure of the exercise. What you give out will come back to you almost immediately. It will be a joy to behold.

6. Harmony

Last, the exercise of Harmony consists of blending the first five exercises into your life in a daily way. As you continue to practice them, an inner balance and equanimity will become regular states in your soul. Calmness will replace inner anxiety and doubt, and you will be able to retain your composure even in the most trying situations. The tendency to swing from the heights of joy to the depths of despair will vanish, and you will have a sense of being *ready* for whatever approaches you from the outside.

These exercises demonstrate that the inner life can in fact determine the quality of your external, environmental life, and you can begin to see that everything that happens does so for a reason. Faith, trust and confidence of purpose will replace doubt, fear and restlessness.

In short, there will be an inner harmony that will put you on top of the world. The voice within will be active and awake, and you will find that people, opportunities and situations will come to you. You have only to do the work on yourself and make the efforts of the exercises for your deepest talents to come to the fore.

You will have made yourself ready to attain what you are destined to attain, and you will find that your potentials are realized rather than imagined.

The entire process of ego development is wondrous, mysterious and fascinating. Love becomes a reality rather than a fantasy. Pleasure takes on a different quality, and sorrow brings with it a certain enlightenment and direction.

Although these exercises are not specifically designed for the Saturn Return years, they are especially helpful for the trials and tests of the years from twenty-eight to thirty-five. They build confidence and purpose and can pay great dividends when the crisis of confidence arises at thirty-five.

The six exercises are building blocks. They produce a rich and cultured soil for the growth of the creative, dynamic individual. They are centering actions which align the inner and the outer worlds in a delicate balance.

CHAPTER SEVEN

Sex and Love—
The Dear Forbidden Fruit

It's easy to fall in love, but much harder to fall out. You remember the first night, the first moment you saw someone special who looked at you as if he cared, and you remember the first time he touched you and kissed you and made love to you, but do you remember when the touch, the kiss, the bodies merging together no longer excited you? No longer meant anything to one of the two of you? No longer had the fire, the tingle, the drive? Yes, beginnings are clear to see; endings are much more murky. Falling in love is spectacular; letting go of love is torturous.

Some single people have trouble falling in love—finding the quality of person with whom they wish to share. Others have trouble falling out of love; they hold onto relationships that are not working simply because of the idea that a bad relationship is better than no relationship. Falling in love and falling out of love are two sides of the same coin because in each condition something is very much at stake within the individual psyche which colors every other action in life.

In many single people there is an emptiness of soul, a deep pocket of loneliness, because the pieces don't seem to fall in place. Either there is no one to fall in love with, no one who meets the "standards," or there is someone who cannot or does not want to make a commitment to a long-lasting emotional relationship. In many cases the single person's love life is a sometime thing, here today and gone tomorrow, as tenuous as a spring flower in an icy rain.

In the face of broken promises and unfulfilled expectations, it's easy to withdraw into indifference, convenient to keep protected, intelligent *not* to give your heart away. Love has never been what it seemed to be, and many singles approach a new emotional affair with trembling trepidation. On one hand, a new love affair would be very nice, but on the other, who needs the aggravation?

So there is a retreat: to an old "friend," to a new apartment in a different part of town, to younger lovers who have not been spoiled and can still take a chance. You begin to ask yourself some baffling questions, facing ingrained patterns which are so easy to repeat and so difficult to change.

Why is it so easy to fall into relationships which go nowhere after a few dates? Why is it so difficult to let go of relationships which you know are not good for you? What is that fear, that shadow, that vague sense that love will never happen again if you don't make it with *this* one or if you let *that* one go?

What is the chemistry of ripe love turned sour or no love at all that makes us face our singleness in terrible and frightening ways? What is really happening when you look in the mirror and wonder why you can't fall in love all the way? Can't give of yourself completely? Can't keep the fire glowing for more than a month or two or three?

What is going on in the psyche, both positively and negatively, when love keeps walking in and out of your life or is not there at all?

What is wrong with you? You begin to wonder about so many near misses and false starts, about the ideas, fantasies and conditions of true love. What is love anyway? Where can you find a clue? Not even an answer. A clue will be most appreciated, thank you.

So somebody gives you the bright idea to look at your track record. To see yourself clearly. To examine your expectations and adolescent concepts of love. To entertain your spiritual as well as your physical plane.

And what do you see in your track record? Track records don't lie.

What my track record clearly shows, says the composite single hero or heroine, is an overconcern with sex and orgasm, a hasty retreat into boredom when the sex becomes routine and the need for a new thrill, another body, another bed, another smell, touch, taste, feel and look almost every month. My track record shows that I like variety, preferring the emotional roller-coaster rides of intense beginnings and slow, painful endings. And still, I keep looking into eyes and over bodies for the secret to my love life. Because love has eluded me for so long, love is the most precious treasure I wish to hold.

There it is—in my track record. Sex and love.

One of the reasons I'm still single, you say, is that I'm fundamentally concerned with sex and love on *my* terms. Sex and love exist mainly as ways of satisfying myself, and because sex and love have *me* at the center, there is always something of self-worth at stake in any sexual, emotional encounter. I want to be wanted. I want to sleep with someone I like, trust and respect. I cherish the idea of waking up next to someone the rest of my life, but I cannot seem to find that special someone.

I would like to believe, you continue, that out there is still someone waiting to make my life meaningful and to supply the delicate balance that I cannot seem to maintain living alone. Perhaps it is easier to extinguish all expectations. Better to tell myself to expect a series of short, temporary involve-

ments. Healthier to level off and read books that stimulate my
mind without any emotional risk. Perhaps it is better just to
accept my own singleness and be grateful for the beautiful
moments that come and go. Maybe I should train myself to
see the beauty of endings as well as the thrill of beginnings.
Maybe I should become a creature of the night, on the prowl,
taking the momentary pleasures now and worry about the
consequences later on. Perhaps what I am looking for doesn't
exist. . . .

Marriage is no answer, you think. A desperate union would
add only more problems. No, I'm not ready to get married,
but I am ready for love. Because of all I went through, I still
think I could give a love that would not burn you, or imprison
you, or manipulate you, or clutch at you, or shackle your feet
in the snares of my own self-interest.

I think I know enough about myself to have somebody to
love and to be free at the same time. I have risen above that
adolescent, immature love which forces its own desires, fears
and fantasies on another person. I now care about the effects
of my action on the other person, not only about my own
needs, wishes and fantasies.

I think I can love all the way, you say. I think all the
failures in the past have given me the strength, courage and
conviction to give of myself totally from the head, heart and
gut. Everything past has been just a prologue. Let the first act
of love begin.

So you think you can love?

Prove it, will come the answer. Soon there will be a
knocking at your door, or a glance at the office, or a smile at a
party. Once you think you are ready for an unselfish, super-
aware, creatively conscious kind of love, you will get the
chance to bring your idea into being.

You will get the chance to take that idea and nurture it or
to fall back into the same tentative gestures and delusions that
have been the pattern until now. The crazily delicious magic

about love—which is so intoxicating, refreshing and absorbing—is that there is something supernatural about it. It's as if something higher *knew* who you were and what you wanted. The situation is provided when you have specified your own intentions and believe in yourself. When love comes to you, everything seems easy, right and wonderful. Love can pick you up to see the best in yourself, not to mention the sense of fate and purpose, all the time. Love brings a special meaning, a dimension that is not present if you are caught going through the motions of an in-between, sometimes-on, sometimes-off love affair.

The difficulty for many single people who hang onto love partners even though they know deep down that "this is not the one" is the unclear vision of sex and love. Some confuse sex with love—that the act of sharing their bodies and beds with other people means that those people love them. Too often, sex is sex and has nothing to do with the finer, supernatural quality of love. If sex is sex, feeding an appetite, without any pretensions of being love, sex is reduced to the level of recreation. Like most recreational activities, sex can become boring, tedious and destructive to the soul if another, more refined, more delicate and ultimately more satisfying plane of action is not introduced.

Many single people report having fallen into bed with a partner long before they ever fell in love. Since they were liberated and hip, sex was a form of getting high, of partaking of the pleasures of the body, which had long been kept taboo. They liked to see easy sex as representing a certain freedom of the spirit. There would be a visceral attraction, a laugh, a convenient bed. Perhaps there were a few drinks, or good smoke, or the chance to take a chance and see what would happen. Sex among some singles can be casual, convenient and cavalier, but the bill always comes.

Nothing about sex is casual.

One day there dawns an entirely different awareness: that casual, convenient, cavalier sex destroys a capacity to love.

Every time you have sex with somebody you not only inter-
twine physical bodies, but you also penetrate psychic bodies.
Every time you arouse the sexual energies you also activate an
invisible, nonmaterial field of action where you leave your
mark even when you are physically apart. It is as if the sexual
act wove people together by some very fine, delicate, barely
perceptible fiber. Breaking the fiber once or twice is painful;
breaking the fiber hundreds of times is damaging to the
psyche. Sex has a way of lingering, a quality of permanent
imprint, an indelible weaving together of destinies—a psychic
fact which many people ignore.

Every time you have sex with another person you leave
something of yourself behind, whether you want to or not. If
you have slept with many people, bits and pieces of your
heart are scattered around who knows where. Casual, cavalier,
indiscriminate sex which feeds only immediate, temporal
appetites actually can destroy your ability to give of yourself
to one special person over a sustained period of time.

For many singles, especially those who have been through a
grueling love match, sex is like temporary enjoyment—something you take because you need some immediate gratification
but which you know is not going to last forever. Relationships
are consciously transitory, fleeting, visceral. You deliberately
do not draw too close emotionally because you know deep
down inside, that you do not belong there. The idea of sex is
to avoid hassle, release tension, cater to "physical" needs and
keep unattached. Commitments are threatening precisely because they ask you to give something more intangible than
your body.

Casual sex separates the body from the soul and the spirit,
yet what are you to do? There are physical needs, aren't there?
Why do you have to love somebody just to sleep with him or
her? Why can't you just enjoy each other sensually and then
let the whole exchange go? Why do you have to become
emotionally involved just because you have sex?

A better question is: Why do you have sex if you know the

person is not someone whom you really want? What compels you to play with fire, especially when you have come to realize that expedient sex amounts to zero anyway? What is it that makes you project your physical needs onto the psyche of another person?

What can be done to channel the sex drive into actions which are satisfying to both you and your partner on deeper levels than the physical?

One of the greatest dangers to become conscious of is the "free-sex" attitude encouraged and espoused by so many of the cheap, slick commercial media enterprises. These magazines, novels and even movies put a premium on the orgasm. They advocate the experience of having sex with more than one person, perhaps at the same time. This "philosophy" encourages people to concentrate on the physical plane of sex, advocating new and intricate methods to "heighten pleasure." Easy sex is good sex. The more, the merrier. The higher, the better.

Somehow swinging—the act of having anonymous sex with a person whom you may or may not ever see again—is an ideal, a technique of exploring "individuality" or expressing "freedom." The swinging single looks to experience many kinds of sexual intercourse; quantity becomes more important than quality, immediacy more crucial than longevity, anonymity more desirable than intimacy.

But isn't there something very dangerous in this line of thinking?

Most single people who passed through the Hunter singles classes thought so. They wanted something more than casual, temporary sexual flings, especially if they had had one or two or three. Establishing an emotional rapport was more important and more elusive than fulfilling raw sexual needs. Most saw through the commercial hype of sex which the mass media push because it sells products. Appealing to the body is much easier than appealing to the mind, but in the long run the mind and the heart offer the greatest rewards.

The invisible, psychological realm ultimately carries more weight than the physical. The more the body is fed, the more gratification it requires. If you get hooked on sex, you can forget about love. Sex demands indulgence; love demands self-sacrifice. Getting the two to come together is still the hope of most single people.

But bringing sex together with love often means *letting go.* It means letting go of ideas, needs and fantasies which have been part of the psychophysical bloodstream since the dawn of your individual consciousness. Letting go of a potential love partner whom you want but who doesn't want you. Letting go of the mysterious drive which sends you back time and again to someone who takes from you and rejects you at the same time. Letting go of the fanciful, romantic notion that someday the prince or princess will come.

It's easy to have the idea of letting go of internal processes which rebound and boomerang back on you with such viciousness and possessiveness, but how can you not pay attention to the flushing of a cheek, the quickening of the pulse, the heat between the legs?

How can you let go of needs which are organic, physical and human?

What is the single man or woman to do about desire, sex and love?

What is the answer to sleeping alone and not wanting to?

Health spas, nightly meditations, spiritual visions?

Creative classes, personal inventory journals and astrological magic?

What can replace a warm, loving body under clean, crisp sheets in your own bed? What is better than that, *really?*

Some people prefer somebody to nobody, even if that somebody is different every day, week or month. Having another body there is better than being alone, but *is having somebody there better than having nobody?*

That is a crucial question to answer in realistic terms, and the answer must then be applied to everyday, real-life situations.

A body is better than nobody, but not when that somebody is there only for convenience. Whenever you are using (or being used by) that other body as a service station, no matter what your age, sex or track record, you are feeding a habit that will eventually grow into an addiction.

One of the most important capacities you can develop as a single person is the ability to pass up convenient, expedient sex. Especially if you are involved in an "in-betweener"—an affair which is hanging on but going nowhere—you have to have the courage to say NO! The longer you stay involved with someone whom you love but do not want to be with forever, the more difficult it is to break away. Letting go of a lover who provides comfort, warmth and occasional passion can prepare you for something better, even if that "something better" first demands a period of celibacy and lonely nights.

Especially in the realm of sex and love which are so highly charged and volatile, one must sit down and face one's responsibility, particularly to the other person involved. There are so many sad stories of cases in which one of the two partners could not or would not let go. One partner is often deceived, used and abused. One partner wants love, time and that elusive "something more," while the other is there just to get laid.

It happens to both men and women. Neither sex corners the market on using the other for convenience, and neither wins the contest. But if you have been through a few sexual war games, you have probably come to realize that satisfying sexual affairs come about only when you do not fool yourself about what you want. Something good transpires when you don't confuse the need for sex with the expression of love and when you are able to refuse casual sex on the principle that easy sex goes nowhere.

Once you can let go of the partner who can provide sex or money but little else, then you have a fighting chance to find someone who can provide both sex and love. This letting-go behavior is complicated by the fear that another interesting love partner will never come along. Letting go is difficult when you are plagued by the idea that somebody is better than nobody, so you might as well hang onto somebody.

That is addictive. That attitude can reduce and limit you to transitory, fleeting, ego-deflating, quasi-love affairs the rest of your romantic life.

But how do you get someone to make love to you—physically, emotionally and spiritually? Is it something that "just happens" in the natural course of affairs? Or is there an internal chemistry, one that can be consciously put into motion based on an idea of how love is conceived, grows and develops?

A good place to begin to unravel this baffling process is to consider what qualities you admire, respect and are attracted to. What is it in another person that lights a fire inside you? Can you discern the inner action behind outer behavior which makes someone special, desirable and dynamic?

If you are like a good number of other single people, you appreciate style, an awareness on the part of the other person of your own needs, wishes and ideas as an individual. You react positively to someone who is relaxed, yet focused, someone who knows what he or she wants and who has developed a center of self-reliance within and therefore will not grasp, clutch or smother you.

There is something very intriguing about someone who has an inner peace, an inner quiet and a daily purpose. There is something mystifying about someone who can be comfortable with silence and who does not have to push, demand or manipulate you into doing what he or she wants you to do, someone who has developed an ability to give you space to grow and experience. More than anything else, the inner sense of quiet is the mark of a person who can love and who can accept love in return.

People are attracted to someone who has a sense of his own individuality which is not imposed on others, to someone who is on target, first within himself, and who can adapt to any situation because there is a basic confidence, a trust and a creative spark that are alive and growing.

Style is developed out of an awareness of what efforts to make as much as out of innate talents, needs and environmental backgrounds. Often there is a mental picture in the inner eye of someone with style—a vision of how he or she wants to be. Once the idea is present in the form of a visualization, there is a very good chance that one can bring the idea into being—if at the same time one keeps inner peace and quiet in mind.

You can get someone to want to make love to you on all levels by being yourself and creating the conditions of love in your own internal and external environments. If you are single and dismayed by the prospects of living without a love partner, there are two definite directions to take, two paths to follow which will merge and blend together somewhere along the way.

First, as has been discussed, you must take time to determine what you want, the nature of your repeated patterns and the specific obstacles that seem to get in the way of your living up to your ideas and potentials. The first direction is inward, in that you must make a commitment to yourself and attempt to call a truce to your own inner struggles.

Secondly, you can create the conditions of love in your own immediate physical environment—in your own living space and in the places you go for social events. It's very important to see your living space as a reflection of your inner processes. If you spend time, money and energy on your own home, you will have a place which is truly your own. You will have something tangible and spiritual to share with another person. In addition, you will have a super place to entertain. If you are someone who has trouble relaxing in public, make the privacy of your home your showcase. The process of maintaining and sustaining your own private living space often extends to public and psychological areas as well.

If you can create a living space that is warm, relaxed and filled with healthy plants, soothing music and good books, a space with a clean, functional kitchen and a mellow, comfortable bedroom, chances are that you will behave positively when in public. Affairs of the heart and soul often start in the home—your own immediate home, not that of your parental past.

Once you become genuinely tuned in to see yourself in your house, you will awaken the ability to find a way to make contact with others on the public front. Once you have an inside track on yourself and can see your reflection in your environment, you will probably become convinced of the idea of a *soulmate*—that there is one person who can extend and complement you and whom you can "see" waking up next to forever. The soulmate is one who seems to know you and speak your language without issuing ultimatums, making demands for unconditional surrender or pulling out at moments of crisis and climax.

Good style often involves this one basic idea: that there is some special person with whom you can build a healthy home and plan for a future. The task then becomes to trust that vision, to relax and enjoy your life while waiting for that person to arrive on the scene. Your task, as one who believes in the concept of a soulmate, is to prepare yourself to face the moment when you are asked to give of yourself totally and completely. When that person does make an appearance, it is your task to recognize the inner and outer qualities and to trust the efforts you have made up to this point. If you lose sight of your *idea* or task, you might demand, push, force or manipulate without even being aware of what you are doing. If that happens, you will very likely scare that special person away. No one likes to be manipulated, especially if so much is at stake. If you are self-reliant and centered within yourself, you can offer and suggest, rather than force or demand. Once you begin the process of listening to your own voice within and listening to others without criticism, you can create a current or open a channel which others can see, feel and *want* to share.

Good style is a matter of awareness—of yourself and your task, of the psychological condition of the other person and of the environmental conditions of the meeting. I like to imagine someone who I think could be my soulmate as a doe in a large, open meadow, just grazing, surviving, looking over her shoulder for signs of danger.

How should I approach that doe in the meadow? How would I tame "a fox"?

There it is—your doe in the meadow or bull in the yard. How do you get that animal to come to you, to have faith in you, to eat the food you offer, to want to see *you* again? What do you have to do to establish the trust out of which true love can grow? How can you create an internal landscape of love?

For me, the answer lies in the realm of ideas and spiritualized thinking. More and more, living single becomes infused with life, pregnant with opportunity, electrified with adventure and saturated with surprises when I keep in mind the idea of a soulmate. When my head is tuned into the invisible plane which includes, yet transcends the physical, I see a reason for being. I see a blueprint to complete. I see a house, with a woman and children, a house to build from the foundations. I see travel, books and plays. I see the world before me and the world after me. Sometimes I see the world above me, and when I do, I have no problem in meeting people, enjoying people or having the opportunity to relate on the most intimate basis.

It's only when I allow myself to get hassled by the pressure of time, or when I make a move based on raw sexual need, or when I lose my faith that there is a master plan that being single becomes vicious, pointless, unbearable. When I can't change the negative to the positive within myself first, I am at the mercy of fears, anxieties and superstitions. When my house is dirty, I hate myself. I have often confined myself in my own prison and threatened to throw away the key.

Luckily there is some inner, invisible, irrevocable force which will not allow me to self-destruct. There is some other presence within me, especially in my struggles with sex and love, which drives me toward the edge of a precipice time and time again. Something hurls me forward recklessly and unintelligently toward the easiest, most convenient, least challenging contact. There is something in me which holds me back, brings me down and throws me to the wolves.

But there is also something in me higher than *that*— something of the soul and the spirit which understands that I can get a reading on myself by observing the effects I have on other people.

If I can get others to relax, to smile, to be themselves and offer their ideas, dreams and feelings, I myself am in a very good place and headed on the right path. Once I can tune into the radar beam which guided and illuminated Rudolf Steiner all the time, I know it is only a matter of time before my soulmate will appear. There's nothing to worry about, nothing to doubt, nothing to fear when I keep tuned into the spiritual dimension. All I am responsible for is my own work on myself. For being an individual. For being single.

I will recognize my soulmate by the signals she sends out: her gentleness, her enthusiasm, her inner quiet, her sense of herself, her physical and emotional style. She will have a profession, a talent which she works hard to refine, and she will have the warmth and the vision to have children.

She will be a citizen of the world, a reader of books, a student of the spiritual element of human affairs. She will trust her intuitions and be attentive to her dreams. She will condition her mind as often as she conditions her hair, and she will be very much like that doe in the meadow.

I have known many women who met my ideal, but most

have run away when I have approached them. Or I have run away when one turned and came to partake of my feast. Perhaps we ran together for a while, my doe and I, but even at this point in my life one of the two of us has retreated to the safety of the woods which are—in the words of Robert Frost—lovely, dark and deep.

But I do have a promise to keep: one to myself, one to my soulmate and one to the Being who is above all this. I will reach for the best within myself. I will go out and try to find, meet and tame the wolf in myself to sleep peacefully with the doe in the meadow.

What are my alternatives—really?

Hot furnaces burn and consume or provide energy for growth. The same energy which creates can also destroy, so it largely depends on where you channel it. The same force within you which hurls you forward relentlessly can also bring the inner peace to sleep with the doe in the meadow.

In some ways, the doe must come to you. You "tame" the fox by having the strength, courage and presence of mind to do *nothing* when it is right to do nothing. If you spend your time, money and energy thinking up ways to trap the doe or ensnare the wolf, the most you can have is an animal in prison, one who will be dreaming of freedom and seeking the best way to get out as soon as possible.

Only your own gentleness, honesty and inner peace will create the conditions of love—the kind of love which is definite, permanent and transcendental at the same time. Listening without criticism, changing the negative to the positive, finding your creative center are not just abstract ideas. The process of nurturing those capacities inside you will attract a certain kind of person outside in the social world.

Work done on yourself at home—homework for yourself and by yourself—sets the stage for your actions in both the public and metaphysical arenas. How you treat yourself when you are alone determines your behavior in public. Since you can clean your house anytime you want, you have a place to start and a very good chance to set up that inevitable meeting with your soulmate.

Learn how to wait and trust.

Learn how to slow down and control appetites.

Learn how to offer rather than to demand.

Learn to see beyond your own desires into the effects you have on others.

Learn to move with the subtle rhythms of timing.

Most important, learn to make sense out of the unexpected. In some way, your every experience has been prepared for by your deeper, unconscious psyche. Therefore, everything that comes to you has a message to give.

Learn to see the extraordinary in the commonplace, the supernatural in everyday happenings, and your soulmate will be much closer than you realize.

Some men and women spend an entire lifetime looking for that special mate, and when the time comes to act—when the doe lifts up her eyes and acknowledges you—it will be your choice whether to stay or run away. Especially at the moment of crisis, what you *do* will count most. You must find a way to bring your ideas into being in the form of an action with feeling, or else you may never see that doe again and spend years looking for another one.

The most exciting feature about being single is that you never know when the doe in the meadow will appear. You never know when someone will sit down next to you at lunch or approach you at the beach or invite you for coffee after a class. All you will have will be your own feelings and some signals from the other person.

If you know what you are looking for, you can recognize the elements and turn on your *positive* energy. If you are in a state of fear, doubt or suspicion, chances are the moment will slip away into the might-have-beens.

Love will always come to you when you are ready.

That seems to be the one true universal law. When you are

ready, you will have the chance to extend, surpass and transform yourself into a divine as well as a human being. Love has that power. It grows when you give it away. It is most wonderful when there is no price tag attached. It is most creative when you are willing to wait and develop stage by stage.

Love is procreative. Sex is often recreative. Both are available. Think about what you want.

CHAPTER EIGHT

Tuning Your Instrument

I had been jogging in the nearby park one Friday evening at twilight when I was attacked by a great hound. A monster Irish wolfhound came loping out of the shadows like some animated fury making playful nipping leaps, intent on taking me along on his joyous romp when his mistress came to my rescue. Assuring me that he would not bite *anybody,* she called him off, and we wound up talking—the lady and I—and walking by the lake, watching the dog make astonishing sprints across the adjacent field. Out of a casual trot, the silver beast with the curled tail would accelerate and leap up straight in the air like a hooked marlin. I marveled at the power, grace and dignity of the dog and at the refined taste of his cool, dark owner, who told me she was a poetess, turned interior decorator.

She laughed easily, with a good sense of herself, and when she invited me to a party she was having the following night, I wondered what she was up to. Just a few people, she assured me, nothing special, something to enjoy, laugh with and let go.

I arrived about eight thirty, and even though I had allowed myself to be half an hour late so as not to be the first one there, I was, in fact, the first one there. Somehow I felt the need to apologize for being only half an hour late, but my cool, dark new friend enlisted me in the final preparations, saying that she was glad I had come early so she could get to know me better before her regular friends came by.

Twenty minutes later several friends arrived at one time, and from then on I was on my own. Her role was to greet and to introduce, and I was struck by the quality of her guests. All the people, both men and women, were in their late twenties and early thirties; all were single; all had some professional, marketable talents. They were making good livings in ways that both stimulated them and paid well. None seemed to need to get married, engaged or otherwise coupled. Although there was an undercurrent of wanting to meet new people, there was no rushing, no pushing, no quick hits—none of the usual behavior I had come to expect from "friendly" encounters of young single people. In short, my task of having a good time was easy to accomplish. Everything was mellow and smooth for about an hour. Then *the* something happened.

A young man in his early twenties entered the apartment, carrying a guitar case. He had long, black, shoulder-length hair and a sullen, intense, anxious-to-please look about him. He wore a Levi's jacket and faded jeans, and without hesitation, as if he were driven by his own private demon, he took a corner of the living room and began banging on his guitar. Within a few minutes all the pleasant conversation in the room stopped short. It was apparent to everyone that this young man had come to take center stage, and it was equally apparent that one of his guitar strings was out of tune. Everybody could hear that his chords did not sound right— everyone, that is, except the young man himself.

He played and played and played, with some passion, with some great sense of drama, with some undeniable force of urgency. Within ten minutes *everyone* had left the living room.

He sat there playing by himself in the dark corner. On the way into the kitchen the poet, my hostess and would-be lover, turned and whispered to me, "Before he sings any more love songs, he'd better learn how to tune his instrument."

Before you sing any love songs, tune your instrument.

A few nights later I discovered that the dark, cool interior decorator was inextricably intertwined with a married man in a tempestuous, self-destructive, self-flagellating affair. The two phone numbers I had jotted down at the party never amounted to anything but a cup of coffee and a boring movie. But the image of that young man, strumming his out-of-tune guitar in the corner of the empty living room, never left me. That picture had staying power for me when everything else had faded.

Was I singing my love songs with an instrument that was out of tune? As with the young man, could everybody else see it but me? Did my own personal passion and need blind me and condemn me to transient, purposeless, indulgent love affairs? Did I *ever* know what I was doing at the moment I was doing it?

That party left me only with food for thought and a great, overwhelming sensation that my own inner instrument was often out of tune, especially when it came to romantic affairs. "Just missing" was not enough for me anymore, and it dawned on me that there is no such thing as being a little bit out of tune. You either are or you aren't. Being in tune with yourself is difficult to measure because it has to take into account the potential and talent of the individual.

Potential and talent—powerful words, dynamic forces, intriguing possibilities: potential and talent. Being in tune was somehow aligned with the *use* of inner potential and talent, so tuning the instrument took a decisively inward turn. I began posing the question of how to tune the human instrument to the groups at Hunter College to see if we could zero in on how to tell if an "instrument" was in tune.

What does tuning the instrument mean? Isn't everyone's

instrument slightly different? What does a tuned human instrument look like in *behavior?* How does he or she operate in everyday interactions—in real time, space and situations?

Although there are varieties of tuned human instruments, there seem to be some basic qualities that are common to exceptional, tuned-in people. Over the years in the Hunter class there developed a pattern of action, a better sense of what a tuned human instrument *does* in everyday behavior. A certain attitude, approach and action link those who are in tune—no matter what the differences in age, sex or conditioning. They share a quality that starts from within and radiates out toward their external world: They attract people for what they are and what they do. The in-tune person *is* what he or she *does.* On the final scoreboard the behavior counts more than the intention.

So what are these basic qualities? How can we spot the tuned-in human being? How can we tune ourselves in to our deepest potentials and greatest talents?

Being Yourself

Have you ever tried to *be yourself* on purpose? What happens when someone is taking a photograph of you? Isn't there usually some kind of inner adjustment, some shifting of the gears, some trying to be something *other* than what you are normally?

Have you ever attended a party where people were *playing at* being themselves and were not aware of what they were doing? Have you ever strolled down a singles beach on a Fourth of July weekend and witnessed the attitudes, poses and tactics that people fall into automatically? Have you ever tried to pick up somebody you didn't know and groped around for the right words, lines and postures?

If you have experienced or participated in such activities, you know that being yourself is not an easy task to accomplish, especially when there is some kind of pressure to perform. We all need approval, attention and admiration, but some of us consistently try to maneuver, plot and coerce others to give us what we want.

Yet one of the most outstanding features about an in-tune person is the sense of being in touch with his or her inner self. The in-tune person seems to be beyond or above playing games to attract others because there is an intuitive understanding that the best way to impress people is *not* to try to impress them. This is a basic paradox of behavior. Sometimes the best possible move is to make no move at all. Sometimes it is best to relax and let the other person come to you, and many men on the make do not understand this simple rule.

When it comes to making contact with a woman, many men will rush, push and expect sexual favors too soon, based on some inflated idea of their own masculinity or of what "real" communication with a woman is all about. Because our society still places a high premium on macho, he-man, rough-and-ready behavior, many men feel they have something to live up to, something to prove, some alarm clock inside which beats away a message to a constant ticking: Get Laid Now.

This something-to-live-up-to syndrome, both in men and in women, is the biggest bugaboo in being yourself. Most often it exists on an unconscious plane so that individuals are not aware of what they are switching on. It is almost an automatic response triggered by deep needs and social conditioning. Very often everyone around except the phony himself is aware of the phoniness of his behavior. He thinks he is doing what he is supposed to be doing, when really what he is supposed to be doing is being himself.

This behavior is extremely subtle and often overlooked as "normal." We expect people not to be themselves and allow for a distance between what a person *does* and what a person *is*. We chalk up game playing and posturing to human nature, the frail and vain streaks in the human composition, yet we often use the behavior of others to justify our own limitations.

We tend to pick friends or public figures as models based on their external behavior alone, but there is always an internal action beneath.

Getting at the internal pattern of action is what being yourself is really about. It is a process of defining your own rhythms, your own values, your own principles and of allowing your inner guide to lead to behavior. In the past decade much of the singles revolution has been concerned with *finding yourself,* with locating a *center,* with an attempt of discovering *who you are* beyond the roles that society has asked you to play.

This move within has been an attempt to maintain integrity as an individual, yet clear techniques on how to be yourself are rarely suggested or presented in an orderly fashion. Being yourself is not as neat and tidy as it sounds because of needs, desires and false models. Yet there are things to do to practice being yourself, techniques to master, experiments to perform.

There are two effective techniques that can help you *be yourself* better. When you feel yourself going through nervous changes as you stand to speak before people you do not know, or when you feel an internal pressure at a party with new people, or when you feel a distance between your actions and your intentions, in all pressurized situations keep the following two ideas in mind:

1. Relax your shoulders and your eyebrows.
2. Talk *to* your listener.

After five years of studying professional acting and directing with a master teacher, I was able to crystallize all his teachings and philosophy into the phrase "Relax your shoulders and eyebrows." Especially when you are feeling something, or when you become nervous, or when you are confronted, if you can remember to relax these two areas of the body, you will be well on your way to being yourself under all conditions.

Why the shoulders and eyebrows? Because psychic and mental tensions hit those two areas first, and tension is the biggest constipator of talent and potential known to humans. When you are tense, you are never yourself. Often you will be tense in these areas without knowing it, so you will *not* be yourself without knowing it. Besides the physical tension, however, there is another psychic effect involved with this technique.

As you remind yourself to relax, especially the mental tension between the eyebrows, you take on a different quality—a relaxed, controlled, spontaneous quality. As you remember to relax, you will find that laughter comes more easily. You'll find new situations less threatening and more enjoyable. You'll often find feelings bubbling up when previously you held them in.

In the fast-paced, hectic, pressure-packed modern world, relaxation is almost a lost art. We tend to dismiss it as unimportant or inconsequential, but the fact remains that we work best, feel more, reach out when we ourselves are in a state of relaxation. The body and mind will not relax automatically. Frequently the body will get tense and the mind will rebel under the pressure of problems.

Relaxation must be a conscious directive at first. You will have to remind yourself to relax your shoulders and your eyebrows very often in the beginning. Just as in driving a car, certain efforts first have to be made consciously before they become natural and automatic. Every time you come to a street corner or stop at a red light, simply check your shoulders and your eyebrows. While you walk down the street, observe the area directly above the nose and between the eyes of pedestrians. Every time you see a wrinkled brow and forehead check your own to see if you are relaxed. Chances are that when you remind yourself to relax your shoulders and your eyebrows, something grand will come to you. Something you have always wanted. Something special.

Talk to your listener, facing the person you are with and

looking at him eye to eye. Have you ever been talked *at?* Since everyone has, you are aware of the difference between being *talked to* and being *talked at* in others, but many people do not know the difference when it comes to themselves. They think they are talking *to* when, in fact, they are talking *at,* and again, this is largely an unconscious process.

Talking to means you are paying careful attention to the person in front of you. You are aware of the other person's eyes, his face, his hands, his gestures, his body language. Instead of imposing your own ideas, feelings and demands on another, you are looking for signals so that you can bring the other person into your orbit. Talking to means being conscious of the inner life of another person and directing your energy out to him.

Talking to is a very valuable trick in new situations. Instead of centering on yourself and worrying about how you are doing, you give yourself an outer focus of attention. When you pay attention to the other person and make an effort to talk to (rather than to talk at) him, he receives a feeling that you care, that you are being personal rather than impersonal, that you are open to listening and receiving, rather than being demanding and imposing. Talking to someone invites him into your orbit, and if talking to is coordinated with relaxing your shoulders and eyebrows, a very interesting and appealing quality emerges. Because most people do not bother to relax their shoulders and their eyebrows, because most people talk at and do not pay attention to others, because most people are unaware of what they are doing at the moment they are doing it, most people do not look as if they are being themselves. Something is a little bit off. Something is out of tune. Something is artificial and superficial.

You, by injecting these two conscious efforts into your behavior, are more relaxed, more in tune, more confident. Something you are doing is, in fact, different, and this "something different" starts to attract other people. Your quality is one of being at home with yourself, being happy

with who you are, unafraid to think, feel and act. There is a
sense of spontaneity, of centeredness, of being on the right
track in those people who practice these two basic efforts.
Once these techniques become ingested and flow in the
psychic bloodstream, being yourself is natural and organic.

Presence of Mind

It was five thirty on a hot Friday in July. The subways were
like cattlecars, packed with sweating, stinking people who had
just completed a day's work and were now being boxcared
home. At the Seventy-second Street station one wave of riders
moved out and another wave rolled in. The train closed its
doors and began to take off. Suddenly screams filled the
station. A woman had caught her arm in the door! She was
outside the car and could not pull her arm out. She was being
dragged along the station platform, and the train engineer did
not know it. She had ten seconds to live.

Dozens of people witnessed the situation, but one Puerto
Rican man fought his way to the emergency switch and
stopped the train before it left the station. While others froze
and looked around helplessly and bewilderedly, this man had
an idea of what to do and did it without wasting time, space
or energy. The situation caught him by surprise as much as
anyone else, but he reacted from an intuitive, immediate grasp
of the moment and saved the life of the woman.

The man displayed what is known as presence of mind,
which is the ability to know what you are doing at the
moment you are doing it. Presence of mind means that there
is an *idea* behind an action, without which behavior is fuzzy,
muddled and without purpose. With presence of mind, an
individual is free to act decisively, immediately *and* emotionally, but with an emotion that has a target and a meaning.

Crisis situations such as the one with the woman on the
subway provide opportunities for the direct and obvious

display of presence of mind, and in that particular situation it was a matter of life and death. Yet presence of mind can also be displayed in everyday interpersonal encounters in an equally striking manner. Presence of mind describes an inner quality of a person, as well as the behavior of a person. The in-tune person radiates a sense of knowing what should be done intuitively, but unlike a crisis situation, this kind of presence of mind is something that can be developed and repeated time and time again.

For example, presence of mind can be practiced by keeping an idea in mind during an entire day. You can direct yourself to enjoy this entire day, no matter what you are doing or whom you find yourself with. You invest your emotional energy in making this idea come alive. Instead of complaining or finding fault, invest your emotional resources in positive, joyful actions. The purpose of the exercise is to give yourself a positive action line to follow and to put something into your day that would normally not be there.

As you practice keeping the idea of enjoying your day in your field of consciousness, you give yourself something to do. This task tends to fill up empty space so that depression, anxiety and loneliness will not crawl in as they do if you give them half a chance.

Presence of mind is a concept related to that of having a task, in that you are consciously putting energy into situations where normally and instinctively you would sit back and react. Instead of letting "them" do *it* to you, you can begin to change the color of your day by what *you put into it* through the nature of your ideas.

In emotional, romantic situations, presence of mind often means learning how to wait, learning not to force and learning to allow another person freedom of expression. As you learn to relax and take time in getting to know another person, as you learn to quiet your impulses to criticize and doubt, as you learn to think of what you can do *for* the other person, then you are closer to attracting the kind of person you are looking for.

In some ways presence of mind is paradoxical. Keeping in mind the idea of taking time lowers the pressure of having to score immediately. Without this pressure, you are able to relax and enjoy the moment more thoroughly. Out of such enjoyment inevitably comes involvement at a meaningful level. As you practice presence of mind, you develop a sense of calm and purposiveness. You become more willing to give, more willing to let go of the fear of rejection, more able to speak and act without hesitation. A person with presence of mind is attractive because there is a unity among ideas, feelings and actions. There is a basic sense of being in touch with the deeper parts of the self, as well as an ability to enjoy all people for what they are as individuals. Presence of mind leads to an ability to harmonize without giving up one's own ideas and values. There is a sense of being in a certain time in a certain place for a certain reason. The person with presence of mind is able to think on his or her feet and express what he or she thinks, feels and wants.

Some people have offered the objection that presence of mind can make a person too controlled, too intellectual, too manipulative. Some people react to the idea of presence of mind as something which will rob them of their own ways of thinking, feeling and acting. But I have found the opposite to be true. Many examples of how presence of mind operates come to mind. A dancer rehearses a choreographed dance again and again to get the *idea,* to develop presence of mind about that particular dance. Knowing the steps, learning the rhythms and the changes, feeling the heart of the music during rehearsals prepare the dancer for opening night. Instead of freezing emotional circuits, careful preparation, presence of mind and knowing what the dance is supposed to be enable the dancer to tap his or her depths in performance. The *idea* opens the soul to emotions; the effect is the opposite of that of freezing the inner life.

One of the best ways to develop presence of mind is simply to practice it during your everyday encounters. Before you go out of the house, say to yourself five or ten times, "Presence of mind." In the beginning, put up little signs where you can see them saying, "P.O.M." Every time your eyes fall on one of the signs, assume that there is a reason for its happening at that moment. Do you know what you are doing at the moment you are doing it? Is there a clear game plan? Are you reminding yourself to keep an idea behind your actions?

At the end of your day, in your journal, let the events pass before your field of consciousness. As yourself: "Did I behave with presence of mind today?. . . Could I have behaved with presence of mind today? . . . What kept me from it? . . . Did I witness anyone else behave with presence of mind? If yes, what were the time, place and situation? If no one behaved with presence of mind today, what would have happened if someone had? How would the quality of the day have changed?"

All presence of mind takes is a heightened consciousness of the moment. By extending your consciousness at any given moment, you feel each day taking on a richer, fuller, livelier quality. Presence of mind adds depth and dimension to what could be flat, dull, routine and takes the sting out of being alone and being single.

Giving yourself something to do, taking the time to check your perspective and reviewing the day from a specific point of view lead to growth, confidence and the courage to be. Joy is available to everyone, especially to singles who can make the time for themselves to understand the basic fact of their existence: that each person is responsible for the quality of his or her own life.

Enthusiasm and Joie de Vivre

Is there anything more infectious than enthusiasm? More attractive than someone who *really* cares about what he or she is doing and about the people who share a common space?

Indifference is one of the biggest, most common and most

destructive pits that a single person can fall into. The sense of not caring, of just living, of going through the motions is one that can creep up silently and without warning, and if there is a sense of being in a rut in your single life, find a way to turn on your enthusiasm fast. Indifference can strangle you into a state of inertia and condemn you to years of remaining in the prison of your fantasies.

One of the hallmarks of the in-tune person is an inner fire, an inextinguishable zest for life, an inner passion which seems to be fed by every action of every day. Because the enthusiastic person knows that indifference is just a special brand of negativity, he or she consciously seeks to send out a positive set of rays and vibrations. At first this positive stream of thoughts and energies must be deliberate and directed, much like learning a new language or coordinating the sheet and the tiller of a sailboat. Experiences and words eventually taken for granted have to be seen and thought of in a new way. One deliberately seeks new points of view, just to keep a freshness and an openness to your daily life.

It's too easy to let yourself fall into a rut and into a depression. But if you make it your business to put an idea into some situation, even one that is painful or tedious, then you can begin to activate your own inner self in a positive, creative way. Creativity is a way out of boredom and can be practiced in everyday, behavioral situations.

For example, suppose you are to have dinner with a friend or a relative who is constantly depressed, always complaining, always criticizing, always wondering why a healthy, attractive person like yourself is still single. Let's assume that this person is always giving you a slight nudge and turning the knife in your back. There is some kind of obligation involved, and you have no gracious way out. It is one of those moments in life when you are squarely faced with the responsibility of family or friendship, even though you are not willingly drawn to it.

How can enthusiasm be turned on in such a moment? What can you do? You have two or three hours of sheer torture in front of you. How can you save the day for yourself, if for no one else?

Slip the old standby into your computer. Give yourself the conscious task of changing the negative to the positive. Instead of reacting to the negativity of the other person, shield yourself by throwing some of your positive energy into the field. Giving yourself something to accomplish takes the emotional weight off your shoulders, and interesting results often take place.

Even if it takes some clever maneuvering, try to have the other person talk about himself or herself as a child or a young adult. Ask about the ideas and the experiences that shaped his life. Ask him who his favorite singer was or what movie star he had a crush on. Ask about the first time he or she ever fell in love. Accomplish your task of changing the negative to the positive by trying to learn something about the other person's inner life while listening without criticism.

Make believe, pretend, suppose—whatever switch you have to flick on—that the person sitting with you at this particular moment in this particular place has a secret to reveal to you. Your "job" is to unravel that secret. Your "mission" is to unlock the door that separates the two of you in psychic space. Your destiny is somehow inextricably linked with this person at this time. Even though you may know you do not want to spend a great deal of time with this person in the future, try making this person feel special and good about himself or herself tonight.

This kind of task, practiced on people you do not particularly like, goes a long, long way when you meet someone who does speak your language and for whom you feel something deep. How you deal with the obstacles, the uncomfortable situations, directly affects the more positive situations that develop in romantic, intimate, emotional exchanges.

This task is particularly effective and important when you find yourself on a date with someone you *know* you will never see again. Circumstance has somehow brought you together. The man or woman appeals to you in no way. In the past you might have looked for the first escape hatch possible to run back to the sanctuary of your bedroom or your favorite bar.

This particular night you are to be a little morbid and to keep your own mortality in mind, as if by some grand design, your exchange with your date were to be the final one in your present lifetime. You can leave the earth on a negative, sour, bitchy note, or you can make your last dance one of grace, charm and beauty.

This image is morose, but it is aimed at a higher state of mind and awareness. If you can imagine a tie between your finite actions and the infinite dimensions of soul and spirit, then you can see how what you do here and now makes a difference in your future life—wherever that might be. Chances are that the idea of your own death will lead to an action different from your normal behavior. You can turn the ordinary into the extraordinary with the power of an idea. This is not to say you are to dwell on the subject of your own death, but keeping it in mind when you have to face a negative few hours always shifts the weight of the moment to a higher plane of concern.

When you are depressed, lonely, agitated, ready to kill, switch on the "This Is My Last Day" button. See what happens in this exchange. For most people, the more the idea of death is kept in mind, the more enthusiasm they have for life and the more precious all exchanges become. This sense of drama, of purpose and of mission can be developed if you care enough. If you have any presentiment that one of your own inner strings is out of tune, know that you are not alone. Know that there is something you can do about it that will trigger your creative juices.

In a paradoxical, yet fascinating way, if you turn toward an idea and away from your feelings in a negative situation, you will feel better. By making another person feel better, you will also be building a talent within yourself. Enthusiasm complements courage, and the more you can keep it in mind, the closer you are to attracting someone special into your life.

Sense of Humor

More than anything else a sense of humor is a way of seeing the world. Like presence of mind and a joie de vivre, it can be developed.

If you can walk, you can dance. If you can laugh at someone else's perceptions, you can have someone laugh at yours. A sense of humor is out of no person's range, and it is a common mistake to believe that someone's nature is fixed and rigid from birth. In fact, there are many psychic potentials available to everyone that few people realize are available to them. Yet there are certain talents that need to be demonstrated only once to be included in the human repertoire. If one man can bend a spoon handle with the power of his concentrated thought, then it becomes possible for every person to do the same. It makes no difference if one tries one hundred times and fails ninety-nine. The one time of success is enough to prove the capacity. Then it is a matter of technique, practice and perseverance.

Even in normal, everyday situations, people are truly funny in their innocence and their unconscious actions. Especially in normal situations, people are funny because of their own involvement, their own seriousness, their own lack of perspective on their actions in the moment.

As one looks for the humor in situations and in his own behavior, a curious note of harmony begins to enter into his field of consciousness. As an individual approaches the point of conscious compassion for others, he is also treating his own inner self with respect, dignity and purpose. The two capacities always go hand in hand. Many people have noticed that learning how to laugh and enjoy is intimately related to learning how to love. Perhaps these capacities go hand in hand, as they both require a certain way of seeing, a certain way of forgiving and a certain way of reaching out to another person because one *wants* to.

Love and laughter, laughter and love. Before the heavy emotional times set in, isn't a good sign of love the ability to laugh with another? Isn't a sense of humor always attractive in someone else? Isn't it always appreciated, admired and accompanied with warm feelings?

Reach out for it. Reach in for it. Sometimes a sense of humor is all we have.

Tapping the Superconscious

Another magnetic quality of tuned-in people is that they have a certain mystique about them. They seem to have a secret for success. They have a knowledge, a talent, an aura which separate them from other people, and although these qualities are intangible and indefinable, there is no mistaking their presence.

Put very simply, in-tune people are in touch with the superconscious realm of being. Just as there is a conscious mind that filters in the outer world through the five senses and just as there is a subconscious mind that lingers below the surface of the waking hours in dreams, there is yet another plane of mind that is available for tapping.

The extraordinary feature of the superconscious mind is that it is available to everyone who summons it into a state of activity. Tapping the superconscious is like plugging into an electrical circuit which easily charges all intellectual, emotional and spiritual batteries immediately and irrevocably.

More and more, psychic researchers are seeing the human psyche in terms of a computer. The individual is constantly being programmed with hidden scripts, on both a conscious and a subconscious level, and behavior is linked to these hidden scripts. You can allow yourself to act out a script written in your early years of childhood, or you can consciously send out scripts to the superconscious mind. Most people act out fixated behavior because the old programs are still running like bad summer reruns.

Yet it is possible to make conscious efforts to reprogram the deeper parts of the psyche, and the procedure is much easier than you might think. The general formula for positive programming is: Make conscious efforts to penetrate the subconscious, thus awakening the superconscious. Once you are in contact with the superconscious, anything and everything are possible. You can summon riches, love, artistic creations and spiritual enlightenment. You can have anything you want—provided you know what you want and provided you keep in mind a certain set of principles and values.

Getting in touch with the superconscious is much like sailing a small boat. You do not impose your rules on the wind and the water. Rather, you becomes acquainted with natural, physical laws. The more you tune into these natural forces, the more these forces work for you.

As in sailing, the first principle is to recognize and appreciate the power available to be tapped. Before anything else, there must be a basic receptivity, an open-mindedness, a willingness to be happy, successful and dynamic. The superconscious is the source of all material and emotional benefits and will give you what you want as you learn to ask, to discipline yourself and to place yourself under its power.

Tapping the superconscious is most apparent when it is engaged in a creative activity. For me, it's writing and singing and playing my guitar. When working on a story or on a chapter of a book, I have learned how to tap the superconscious, and when I am writing well, "I" am not writing. Something else, some outside force, is working through me. In effect, I become a channel, a receptacle, a faucet. I myself do not create. I allow ideas, feelings and forms to work through me.

This is done by sending out for an image to ground my idea

in a specific time, place and situation. This sending-out procedure is simple and direct. I quiet my mind, shut off the internal dialogue and make the movie screen of my mind a blank. I then ask the superconscious to lead me to an image. Three or four times just before sleeping and just after waking, I ask for some signal, some incident, some feeling to spark the creative flow. Then I let go of the request. I don't dwell on it. I don't hammer it in or hound it to death. In effect, I program my deeper psyche for an answer to the problem. I let the superconscious do the work.

After, I have made the conscious effort to penetrate the subconscious, my job is to keep inner silence during the events of the day and to observe what happens in detail. By looking carefully at the external forms of behavior and the internal chemistry of everyday events, I discover what I am looking for. Inevitably the return on such an investment comes in about three days.

Within three days something will happen in the circumstances of business, or a scene will unfold in a social setting, or a friend will drop a line in conversation which will jump out at me. My request will be answered in some unexpected, often bizarre way. If you consider ideas and feelings to be real, the answer is always manifested on a tangible plane. If you give substance to your own feelings and ideas, if you take those feelings and ideas and intuitions as messages from higher spheres, then you can receive inspiration from ordinary events.

In the ordinary you will perceive the extraordinary. In the commonplace you will detect the artistic. In the marketplace you will find the value of focused energy.

As you learn to quiet your mind, listen without criticism and observe in detail the inner workings of outer events, you can tap the superconscious realm. You can write your own book. You can have what you want when you want it. Love can enter your life, just as you have always wanted, if you cultivate your own inner soil.

It is extremely important to keep an open mind. If you cut

yourself off in prejudices, worries or past failures, you lose yourself there. But once you set out on the process of nurturing your own inner peace, then surprises and events come tumbling into your life on schedule. Know your high tides and low tides, and keep especially alert at two special times: just before sleeping and just after waking.

At these times the channels to the superconscious are most active and charged. The psychic receivers are most tuned then. Formulate precisely what you want. Write it down on paper. Visualize it in your mind. Request that it be materialized and then let it go.

Inner silence is essential. Keep a book on your actions. Learn to think in pictures. Learn to confirm and be thankful. Tapping the superconscious always involves a spiritual growth and awareness which leads to deeper, richer, qualitatively different experiences on the material plane. When one begins to entertain the spiritual dimension, seeing the idea behind *every* material event, one begins to attract all the riches that the material plane has to offer. Instead of being withdrawn and desperate about being single, it is possible to turn that state of being into the most important feature of your existence. As inner capacities become more conscious through the practice of inner silence and presence of mind, your destiny can come under your control. You do not have to be at the mercy of other people, situations or events. You can create your destiny from within—what meets you from the outside is fate.

Almost inevitably it becomes the responsibility of the single individual to work on his or her inner life consistently and consciously. When that work is in progress, as soon as it starts, the spiritual dimension takes on a new life and a force that is as amazing as it is enchanting. Meaningful relationships spring up in strange places. Little moments become pregnant with significance. Coincidences seem as if they are planned on some higher level. Each day is a turn-on when the plug is in, as if one were being electrically charged.

There are specific steps to take to tap the superconscious plane. First, *write down* what you want—ranging from money to creative employment to intimate love—and *visualize* specific pictures. These efforts are veritable keys. Writing down and visualizing are by no means arbitrary just as the rules of the road are not arbitrary in sailing or in physics. The two crucial times of the day are just after waking and just before sleeping. By consciously making the efforts to write down goals and visualize pictures at these specific times, you are carrying out step #1 of the procedure.

The second step in the formula is to pay attention to your dreams, feelings and life circumstances. As if every event held a secret message, look especially carefully at what is happening inside you at night. It is a good idea to keep a dream book by your bed when you are consciously sending out for answers. Dreams often offer specific numbers, symbols and situations which will be the key to solving your problem and reaching your goal.

Step number three consists of *having the faith to let go.* Once you have set the program in motion, you must clear your channels of worry, anxiety and concern. The superconscious is infinite in its resources and will respond *if you do not get in your own way.* Letting go and leaving yourself alone are the key elements in this step of the process; that is why it is so difficult for so many people.

What Can I Do for You?

The marketplace is the testing ground for all new products and academic theories, and relationships with other people, people you do not know well, provide the acid test for the single person. As the years roll by and one is still single or becomes single again, ways become set, and soon all new people seem to have something wrong with *them.* On the first or second meeting, new clothes and harmonious masks are thrown up as disguises and masquerades. Everyone puts his or her best foot forward, but when it comes time to give, to compromise, to make adjustments, many single people retreat to old attitudes, withdraw to old expectations and cover up in old fantasies for safekeeping.

In many parts of the country, many singles experience the phenomenon of the group house. In summer, group houses can be found in the mountains or at the seashore. In the winter, skiing houses are the sites for a meeting of the bodies, sometimes the minds, rarely the hearts. Out of the deep-rooted need for human contact, the inner magnetic pull to meet someone to love, singles give up the conveniences of their own personal space to share a new environment with others. Inevitably nerves are singed, psyches are wounded, yet people come back for more.

The congeniality rating of such group houses is high for about three weeks, and then character traits surface and battle lines are drawn. Sometime near the Fourth of July or just after New Year's, people begin to see in others the reasons why the others are still single. Sometimes they begin to look at themselves with an objective eye and begin to wonder if there *ever* will be someone to live with, love and respect in a day-to-day way.

In such houses, arguments can spring up over practically anything—who ate whose food, who cleaned the dishes and who didn't, who plays the radio too loud in the morning. Petty situations become major sources of confrontation, and in the heat of an exchange with someone you have hated from the start, you can often see a picture of yourself that is startling and depressive.

If, for example, there is one bicycle that "belongs" to the house, and two people want to ride it at the same time, the quality of the exchange at that moment can reveal the readiness of each party to deal with a love affair of depth and meaning. If the exchange happens to be between a man and a woman and if it degenerates into a shouting match, resulting in distance, silence and imaginary conversations with oneself while running on the beach three hours later, something is very wrong.

When the crisis comes, the in-tune person is ready, willing and able to *extend* himself or herself to the other, acting upon one of the most appealing characteristics of a balanced individual: *What can I do for you?* In a confrontation over a bicycle or a messy kitchen, what is really at stake? Control? Domination? Ego? Immediate gratification?

There is a fine line between extending oneself and being taken advantage of. Only the thinnest of hairs separates one who is in control and one who is a puppet. Extension of the self is a highly refined balancing act which can be perfected if at least one person keeps in mind the idea of *What can I do for you?*

What you can do for another person is not always what the other person *wants* at the moment. Often the principle of *What can I do for you?* means saying NO! loudly and clearly, rather than swallowing the emotions and letting the moment slip by. The awareness of *What can I do for you?* is simply a perspective from which to gauge an action. It doesn't mean bending over backward to live up to someone's expectations, but it does mean considering the other person as well as yourself.

Whenever you feel angry, about to be rejected or intimidated, whenever you feel your rights are being ignored or whenever you are aware that you are feeling *anything,* ask yourself the question "What message is this feeling bringing to me?"

As if the feeling itself carried significant information with it, try to capture at the moment the meaning of the feeling. As if something higher were trying to tell you something about yourself and the process of your growth, make an effort to be open and to receive the "message."

If you are like a majority of singles, you tend to repress your feelings and swallow them. In the experience of those who have practiced this particular form of presence of mind, an interesting phenomenon occurs. Feelings become voices which find expression more openly and directly. The inner life has a way of coming to life at the moment. Behavior seems to be more natural and less cerebral, more joyous and less inhibited.

"The only way to have a friend, is to be one," said Ralph Waldo Emerson.

The only way to have a love, is to be one.

Appreciate the Aesthetic

Natural phenomena like the phases of the moon or a landscape that changes with the seasons are good subjects for mental picture taking, but so are people. For those who live in the city, an interesting mental exercise is to take mental pictures of a friend or someone you work with at different times of the day. Using your eyes as a camera, take several stills, and then roll back those stills at night.

Just by taking the time to take such pictures, the inner life of the subject comes alive in a very real, yet intangible way. Both the subject, who doesn't have to know he or she is the subject, and the mental picture taker gain more active, dynamic inner lives, and this process of mental picture taking leads to the voice within.

Another way to learn the secret language of the heart is to take up an artistic activity. Painting, singing, dancing, sculpturing—any activity which asks you to do something, to create something out of nothing, to activate your inner life will lead to the secret language of the heart. It is never too late to start to take classes in any of these activities, never too late to follow an inner impulse, never too late to begin to do what *you* really want to do.

What do you want to do? That is the million-dollar question. Once you have even an inkling about what that something special is, go to it, step by step, stage by stage, knowing that the process is what is important. People have been known joyously to play the piano, entertaining friends at parties and at home, after practicing twenty minutes a day for a year.

Sing, dance, play. Make that a part of your day. Seek the aesthetic, the joyous and the beautiful. It's all there for the taking, and if it's not there for you now, go back to what you want.

Knowing what you want is more than half the battle.

CHAPTER NINE

I Offer These Seeds
for Your Feast

The most a book like this can do is provide food for thought and some practical methods to make dead time come alive. What is most depressing to most single people is the feeling that their lives are incomplete. Pieces are missing. Something available to other people is somehow eluding them. They want to give, love and share, but they find themselves more and more alone. They don't want to be alone, but they don't know what to do to attract loving partners.

Nothing much positive happens out of such a depression unless the blue feeling serves as a motivation to work on the inner self. For a good number of single people, work on the self starts with a definition of wants, a commitment to self-analysis and an ability to relax and act with grace under emotional pressure. We all have feelings, wishes and desires to contact other people, but how we translate those inner activities into behavior is the crucial test.

The idea of a task is very helpful in making such a translation. Giving yourself a task to perform means keeping an idea in mind *while* you are behaving. For many single people, the task of having a good time and making someone else feel relaxed leads to a positive result. When you are consciously working on a task, you can better coordinate the feeling level with the mind level. In fact, keeping a task in mind often helps you relax and be on top of the moment, rather than allow the moment to overcome you.

The following rhyming couplets all imply tasks to try in your own interpersonal relationships—at home, at work, at singles functions where you know no one. They provide a kind of dos and don'ts list which is not meant to be rigid. There's nothing of the Ten Commandments about them, but they do lead to a certain level of awareness and style when they are kept in mind while you are behaving, especially when you are feeling something.

None works without practice. The lessons to be learned in keeping these thoughts conscious as you interact with others enable you to act with courtesy, awareness and intelligence while you refine some of your own innate talents. If you take your time and enjoy these tasks, you will find yourself being more at home wherever you go.

Try not to start and stop. Look over these tasks (and your own) day by day. Try them all, but find the ones which work best for you. Chances are your day and your life will be full of pleasant surprises.

I offer these seeds for your feast.

> The gardener who cultivates the soil,
> Plants the seeds and weeds the garden
> Does not pull out the sprout
> every day
> To see how it's doing.

The Sprout Is In:	*The Sprout Is Out:*

When you reach for
  what is best
	When you retreat
	  from every test

When you laugh
  at what you do
	When you lunge at
	  someone new

When your body
  is in tone
	When you cannot
	  be alone

When you see ahead
  a year
	When your goal
	  is lost in fear

When you learn to wait
  with trust
	When you feel love
	  is a must

When you look for
  what is good
	When your favorite word
	  is should

When you sense
  the stars above
	When you think
	  that sex is love

When you entertain
  perfection
	When you seek
	  or fear rejection

The Sprout Is In	*The Sprout Is Out*
When you learn to be alone	When you never are at home
When you profit from your pain	When you always seek to gain
When you value what's within	When you dream of could-have-been
When you focus on a task	When you don't know when to ask
When you like to take a chance	When you find you're in a trance
When you trust your intuition	When you doubt your precognition
When you want to be a friend	When you never can extend
When there's balance in your center	When you hesitate to enter
When you're willing to believe	When you judge and don't receive

The Sprout Is In	*The Sprout Is Out*
When your quality is gentle	When your actions all are mental
When you're thinking while you're speaking	When your interests are self-seeking
When you keep yourself in health	When your driving force is wealth
When you find a long-range plan	When you expect a perfect man
When you remember to give thanks	When you justify your pranks
When you learn to let pain go	When you get angry for a show

Flying solo is an attitude about yourself, a perspective about inner and outer events and a way of approaching people, places and time. As it leads to graceful behavior and a positive frame of mind, flying solo is a philosophy of living. It places the responsibility of your life squarely on your own shoulders while pointing toward higher, more subtle, less tangible powers, which guide, protect and give hope to an otherwise fearful and lonely existence.

As you incorporate the idea of flying solo into daily behavior, a certain trust and confidence builds up in the inner life—a trust in efforts rather than in results. Once the proper efforts are made and you recognize the process in the pattern of events, a freedom is born within that enables you to involve yourself deeply with daily life. As you take time to define and refine daily and life tasks, you become more at home with yourself no matter where you go. Because there is a certain readiness to take a chance and risk commitment, you tend to meet others everywhere while you nourish a few special relationships. As thinking becomes coordinated with feeling and willing, you become more open, more attentive, more attuned to the opportunities and the alternatives available. Enjoying flying solo makes you receptive to many planes of reality.

The idea of flying solo is a powerful force which affects the quality of daily life because it builds resiliency and a sense of purpose. It puts a different frame around the picture of daily events.

"Going it alone" demands courage and a total commitment to yourself which, in fact, build the capacity to love and share with other people. No other person can make your life complete, and as long as you look to the outside for meaning and satisfaction, you will be at the mercy of circumstance. You can best meet other people by first meeting, enjoying and loving yourself because the fundamental puzzle lies within. The pieces are all there. It takes trust and love to fit them together.

The idea is to cherish this time of being single as an opportunity for self-exploration, self-commitment and self-growth in a creative sphere. What you do when you are alone often determines the quality of relationships you have in public. As a single person you have the time to determine what you want, the chance to define some guiding principles of behavior and the opportunity to shoot for what is best and highest within yourself.

Flying solo does take time to develop, but especially if you are single and are looking for something more, it is the only way to fly.

CHAPTER TEN

The Next Time Is the First Time

The next party, the next weekend, the next class, the next telephone call might very well be the first time love ever walks into your life. No matter what has happened to you before, *the next time is the first time.*

This attitude, the very idea that the next time is the first time carries with it a powerful force—a force which can make *the* crucial difference in your enjoying or despairing about your future years. Once you, as an autonomous individual, "get the idea" that your ideas, your attitudes, your energies actually shape and determine the quality of your everyday life, then you can be well on your way to attracting the people, events and situations that will allow you to live up to your greatest potential.

Relationships, like civilizations, rise and fall on moments— fleeting, unexpected exchanges—in which glance and gesture often speak more eloquently than any word or proclamation. All moments have an inner chemistry, a psychological preparation. Nothing ever just happens by itself. Not love, not disaster, not happiness, not unhappiness. Behind all such conditions lies a force, an energy, an impulse which can be channeled and guided by anyone who really wants to—by anyone willing to make an open-minded, persevering commitment to the development of the inner psychic life. No matter what your age, sex or romantic track record, it is never too late to develop positive attitudes, like *the next time is the first time.*

When the crisis comes, as it inevitably does to everyone who reflects on his or her life, your relationship with yourself is all you have. What you, as a single individual, do *now* will make all the difference when the emotional heat is on. It's at the crisis moments that positive attitudes become most functional. When the pain is real and deep, when there seems to be nowhere to turn, where there seems to be *no next time,* then it is time to turn on the big guns. It is time to listen to your quiet self, your voice within, your heart and soul.

The following story occurred during the summer in Amagansett, New York, a beach resort with a deserved reputation as a singles summer colony. In a difficult, painful, joyous and wonderful way, this true life story of Janet Lugano illustrates what it really means to fly solo.

As with all turning points in human lives, Janet Lugano's had a definite before, now and after. This particular incident occurred eight days after the Great Blackout of 1977 in New York City, where areas of congenital, chronic neglect erupted in looting and lawlessness and where the police shot nobody. The blackout was a perfect and necessary backdrop for the crisis of Janet Lugano because when the lightning hit the wires and dominoed down to black out a whole civilization, there followed a weeklong heat wave that engulfed the entire continental United States.

New York suffered under temperatures of 102 and 104 degrees. Forty-four of forty-eight mainland states sweltered under 90-plus heat. For a few days and nights, many eyes and hearts were turned upward in almost cosmic supplication, wondering *why* all this was coming down on us now.

The heat was on—on many levels—and Janet Lugano, a twenty-three-year-old occupational therapist on a two-week vacation before starting a new job, fled to Amagansett to beat the heat and to find a new man to love. Janet had a fierce intensity within her and a street knowledge about her. She had been on her own for a number of years, had lived with a man and had chosen to travel alone. She had a deep need to love and to be loved, a deeper need to be heard, respected and acknowledged as an individual and a still deeper need to find herself, be herself and extend herself to those less fortunate.

Janet was an extremely attractive, feminine woman with a strange air of authority about her. She had thick, flowing hair, dark, flashing eyes, a gorgeous body and an energy that beamed out like a beacon in the dark.

Then there was her hand—her right hand—which almost ruined it all.

Janet had been born with a withered, gnarled, grotesque right hand. The fingers were shortened and swollen, half the length of normal fingers. From the moment of her first breath, she had to live with her hand. She could have had plastic surgery or an amputation so a cosmetic hand could have been fitted for beauty, but she chose to keep her hand the way it was—deformed but functional.

All during her schooldays she fought for her integrity and her beauty as a female, yet while she vacationed at the seashore, in search of that special love she so passionately believed in, the hand surfaced to haunt her.

Janet had been through five or six men on the beaches of the Hamptons during her two weeks. Every man turned on to her body and her energy, but either she devoured them with her need for love or they held no psychological interest for her. They all faded into bodies and poses—all except for one.

He, too, was on vacation. He too, was looking for the perfect score. The summertime fling. The hot, juicy flesh to satiate his basic needs before the everyday routine of the office ate him up again. They bumped into each other on the beach.

They swam, and jogged, but he didn't look at her closely enough to pick up her hand.

She always kept it half hidden. Her Roman beauty and her highly charged energy field acted as a shield, and so a few hours after they met, he invited her to spend the weekend with him on Block Island off the eastern tip of the Island. They left each other in late afternoon to pack in their respective lodgings, agreeing to meet for dinner and a romantic walk along the shore, complete with a skinny dip under a provocative half-moon.

Janet was very excited about the Hollywood ending to her summer vacation. Having just broken up with a man who did not love her "all the way," she wanted very much to be made to feel special and feminine. She was so excited, in fact, that she threw her only set of car keys in the trunk and closed the door before she realized what she had done!

There she was, 8 P.M. on a Friday evening, a couple of hours before her romantic rendezvous and her departure to Block Island, and she was stuck with no way to move. All her clothes were locked in the trunk. The only locksmith was thirty miles and $50 away. Far in the distance a huge thunder and lightning storm was spitting and flashing, heading straight for Amagansett.

The rains that poured down under the great cosmic light show were worthy of King Lear on the moors. There was a flood of thunder, heat lightning and water. When it was all over, after the locksmith arrived and wrestled with the Toyota trunk for a couple of hours, after all that was left of the storm was a clean, fresh ozone smell, Janet met her new man for the grand finale.

At two o'clock in the morning there was a timid knock on my door, followed by a more forceful one, then by a demanding one. I turned on the bed lamp and shuddered. There was Janet Lugano standing at the door in a beautifully embroidered white dress bug-eyed in horror as if she had been chased by a ghost! This lovely, sensuous, sensitive, intuitively alive young woman stood trembling in a state of shock, as if she had witnessed her own beheading.

I sat her down. As soon as she began to tell me what had happened, she doubled over with hurt, head between her knees. She sat sobbing for fifteen minutes. At dinner, she related, the Block Island man noticed her hand. A few minutes later he excused himself to go to the bathroom. When he came back, he said, "I just saw your hand. I can't stand it. I can't stand to look at it. It made me sick, and I don't want to go to Block Island with you."

Not to give him any satisfaction, Janet shrugged, smiled and told him that it would be his loss. She stood up and walked out of the restaurant. As soon as she reached her car, hot, sharp knives began slicing through her entire body, and she felt as if she were being cut up in a hundred thousand pieces.

"Why, why, why, God? Why did this have to happen to me?" She turned on me and my ideas and my book about being single. "Why would I choose this for myself? How did I program this shit for myself and for what reason? *Why* do I have to go through this? Why don't you *answer?*"

I reached out and touched her forehead, her shoulder, then finally held her hand in mine. Her body was shuddering and jerking in sobs. I tried to absorb some of the pain by touch. Nothing was clear to me. The immediacy of this human being convulsing in torment silenced all platitudes or flip formulas. Her pain was real and vicious, and all I could do for the moment was be there and hold her hand.

Because she was experiencing a moment of emotional upheaval, I made it my task to stay with her and talk quietly, but all I could "see" in my mind's eye was a picture of a tremendous crash, a car going out of control on a wet and slippery racetrack. The image was so overpowering that I spoke to her about it.

"It's your recklessness in love that's coming back at you," I offered. "Your need to be wanted, admired, loved and desired. You met this man, wanted to have a big ending to your

vacation, then agreed to go away with him before you knew
anything about him. You set this up for yourself because you
rushed yourself and put your emotional safety into the hands
of an unknown character."

"But what else am I supposed to do? Have three dates
before I make a move? Can't I have a good time? I don't
understand."

"But don't you want someone special? Someone to love *you*
in spite of your hand—*because* of your hand? Don't you want
someone to love you and want you for your talent and
sensitivity? Don't you really want something more than a good
time?" I asked.

She didn't answer, but she was listening. The sobbing
stopped.

"I think you want somebody special—somebody special to
love you the way you want to be loved and the way you
yourself are capable of loving. That person is not going to be
easy to find, and you have to take more care about where you
invest your emotions, energies and especially your body. The
more you go jumping into overnight affairs just to have a
good time, the farther away you'll be from the man you really
want and need."

Nothing more was said for fifteen minutes. No more
convulsions. I could tell that she was thinking.

"But *why?* Why this self-destruct mechanism inside me?
Why do I do this to myself? What drives me to this pain?
Why do I have to live with *this* hand? What is the *purpose?*"

"As far as I can tell," I answered, "it's to get you closer to
yourself. To know yourself from the inside. To gain the
strength that can keep you in balance no matter what happens
on the outside. There's a crazy, unconscious chemistry inside
every one of us, something happening on a level which we
don't see in everyday life. A jolt makes us look at ourselves in
a dramatic way. We bring the jolt on ourselves because of the
thoughts, needs and wishes we send out and generate all the
time. These thoughts have a life of their own, and in a funny

way we create our own world all the time without knowing what we are doing. The experiences we have on the outside are mysteriously connected to what is happening on the inside of us."

"But I don't like to look at myself," Janet interrupted. "I know I'm not going to like what I find there."

"How do you know that?" I asked. "In my experience the hidden psyche is a creative force. The more you tap it, the more it works for you, *with* you. You certainly didn't create this circumstance for yourself on a conscious level, but I'll be willing to bet that it's happening for some reason which you programmed for yourself without knowing it. What are you *feeling* now? What are you thinking? What's running through your head?"

"I'm feeling stupid," she said. "But there's something in me that hears what you're saying. Something about it makes sense to me."

"I think it's happening to make you *see,* to be more careful. To recognize that your dire need for love can be channeled better."

There was another long pause. A deep sigh. Then Janet began to speak.

"The crazy thing is I knew better. I know that I need to do more work on myself as an individual before I can really love a man. I know better, but when I felt afraid and lonely, I went against myself. I've done it before, and I'll probably do it again." And she laughed.

We both had our eyes closed, and we both were floating in that special limbo between sleep and wake. We were holding hands in a place neither of us called home, yet we were together. The entire mood was surreal, otherworldly. The heavy thunderstorm had broken the long heat, and a slight chill filled the air. Just when I thought I was asleep, I heard myself talking. I was startled because I had the eerie sensation that another voice was speaking through me.

"What is at stake is your *freedom,*" I said, "freedom to

choose, to act, to channel your needs into a higher level of concern. This pain is for the sake of your personal, individual freedom. When you work on yourself, you will receive what you are destined to receive. The key is patience, perseverance and courage. Nothing will reveal itself to you if you do not love it, and you will not be able to love anybody else until you treat yourself with love."

"But am I responsible for what I was given at birth? Did I really choose to live a life with this hand?"

"Suppose that you did. Suppose you did have something to do with the body you have. Your body is not as important as your reaction to it. Maybe the whole point is to learn to live with it and not to fight against it. To cooperate and accept rather than to fight and begrudge. You have to develop your inner resources because of your hand, so in a way it is a great gift."

"I'll never see it as a gift," Janet said, and with that I offered her a sofabed in the living room to sleep in overnight. Five minutes later she was asleep.

The next morning Janet woke up in a good mood. She bounced out to the store and made us breakfast. She had two days of her vacation left, and she decided to relax and do nothing. Take a bike ride. Jog along the beach. Take a ride to Montauk for the sunset. Something for herself.

About 11 A.M. she was sitting on her bike outside a bakery in town, nibbling at a piece of black string licorice. Without doing anything, without turning on any charm, without any sexy moves or cute lines, Janet was approached by a man whom she had never seen before.

A local man by the name of John Caldwell stopped a conversation he was having with a friend and began talking to her. It turned out he was a fisherman by trade and an adventurer by heart. A handsome thirty-four-year-old, he would take his seventy-foot commercial boat out into the North Atlantic off the coast of Nova Scotia for ten days at a time, bringing back a catch worth thousands of dollars. He had encountered whales, marlin, mako sharks. He had navigated the dark and dangerous Amazon River.

Everywhere he went he would approach local inhabitants and say, "I know nothing of your customs. I apologize for my ignorance, but that is why I am here. I want to learn about how you live your life." John had trained himself to reach out, to take chances, to be taught, to learn something from everyone he met. He was a world traveler.

John spoke simply, directly, with the authority of practical experience. Everything about him was *real,* and the vivacious Janet was swept off her feet. He bounced his four-wheel-drive Scout over the dunes to hidden beaches that only the local fishermen knew about. He told her stories that kept her entranced for hours.

"He was the reason I came to Amagansett," Janet said. "There would have been no John if I had been on Block Island. Events conspired to bring us together."

John found Janet when she wasn't looking. At the very moment when she had decided to take the day for herself, a man approached her. The events were so intense, so compact, so obvious that she, as participant, and I, as observer and witness, were amazed and incredulous at the flow of the action.

"The toughest thing for me to do is to wait, to believe and trust that whatever happens happens for a positive reason. Sometimes I get crazy thinking I will never find someone to love, someone who wants me for who I am." John called in the fall, visited a few times, then drifted away. He remained as a positive memory for Janet.

It is very easy for all of us to get "crazy" waiting and trusting if our perspective is lost. Many single people "go crazy" when they lose sight of the inner chemistry of their individuality. Being single is a time to uncover, define and refine personal, intangible resources, a time to learn to be at home with who you are as an individual.

That is why courage, fearlessness, patience and perseverance are more than just words to the successful single person. Everyone has a built-in obstacle to overcome. For Janet Lugano the obstacle was her withered right hand. For others it might be a drunken father, a careless mother, an insensitive teacher, an impoverished background. Every person has his or her own withered right hand. If that withered hand results in a basic *fear* of the unknown, in a dependency on outside sources for happiness, in a sense of worthlessness as an individual, that single person is in for a very difficult time.

Yet everyone has the opportunity to deal with his or her own inner life in a positive fashion. Being single provides the perfect setting for the development of thinking, feeling and willing. Everyone reaches the point in the course of normal day-to-day living where everything that meant *everything* seems like nothing. Every material comfort, every insurance policy, every dream of what *should* be are stripped away. Many single people, both men and women, report experiencing that horrible but necessary moment when the ground disappears from underfoot, when every action seems to be encased in a dream, when nothing seems real but thoughts, feelings and wishes, and even they lack material substance.

This experience, unsettling as it is, actually indicates a significant stage of development because it is a crossroads. At that point in the road—and it may last for years at a time—a single person will experience the overpowering sensation of being alone, totally alone in the world. There will be no place to turn except to the life within the self. If the inner life has not been developed with care, patience and perseverance, the individual will be in for a tremendous shock.

If, however, a person has *willed* himself to develop self-reliance, presence of mind and courage in the face of the unknown, then a new field of opportunities and experiences opens up. Another level of being opens up—the level of love.

On an inner plane of action the psyche seems to *create* moments where we have to face up to the basic fact of human existence—that each of us is a separate entity in and of ourselves. We are all alone as individuals, but together in our aloneness as human beings. We can help one another because we know we are alone, but each one of us must do our work for ourselves. At the moment of death we are all alone, facing what we have done as individuals. There is no place to hide, no excuses to be given, no sanctuary where the negative parts of our being can safely retreat.

Because love is the ultimate expression of freedom, it is also the ultimate act of commitment. Unless there is a center, a core, a foundation built on inner spiritual principles of human freedom, love seems to die. Before love comes knocking on your door, there must be someone at home to receive the message. The magical effort in attracting love is learning to live with, by and for yourself first.

The conditions of love can be created! Focused work on the self to develop clear, logical thinking, balanced, refined feeling and firm, purposeful willing is much like cultivating the soil for a beautiful, delicate plant to grow. There is no getting around *effort*. Success in love, like self-fulfillment as an individual human being, depends more on conscious effort than on anything else.

Perhaps being single is a metaphor for being human. We have lived through the assassinations of the 1960's. We are living with the inflations of the 1970's. We are approaching the 1980's with cities rotting from neglect and with energy supplies wasting away. There is not much we as individuals, can do but clean our own house. There seems to be only one way to turn. The external, circumstantial environment offers only occasional thrills and fleeting pleasures, while the inner life is the great new frontier. The telepathic, the intuitive, the psychic, the creative planes have rarely been explored and investigated with any degree of seriousness or commitment.

Yet it is precisely this inner life which holds the key for the quality of life in the next decades. Behind the assassinations, the inflations, the ever-increasing divorce rates, the ubiquitous male-female struggle for power, the roles that society sets up for us to play, behind *everything* is the need for a whole new generation of souls to be free.

The need to be free, the need to be me, the need to be all that I can be is a force finding expression in more and more hearts. Fortunately this need for freedom points to a higher plane of action than the need for sex, pleasure or egoistic gratification. Since freedom of self-determination is won only after a series of tests, trial and tribulations, it is available only to those who entertain and act on the principle that actions are shaped, focused and motivated by ideas rather than by impulses and that lasting values are more substantial than temporal comforts.

It is not easy to be single—to be an autonomous, self-willed, self-reliant, self-activated human being. Especially in a society that still casts stones at the single person and sees individuality as something threatening, it is not easy to see the long-range positive elements about being single.

It's not easy to be yourself, to be single, but it is much easier than most people think. The fear of being alone, the fear of facing the unknown, the fear in cleaning out the closet is always greater than the actual act. Because fears about being single have so much to do with self-worth and self-respect, these fears always come true before wishes, dreams and ideals. The first place to start to make a significant change in style of living is in the realm of attitudes, fears and anxieties about who you are and who you are supposed to be.

Facing the fears within squarely—especially those about being single and alone forever—can open up some *positive* inside tracks into *positive* self-image. Some people find being single is a time of *preparation,* a time to gather the fruits of a variety of experiences, to watch children playing on the seashore and envision a few of their own. Being single gives you the opportunity to question what is real and what is not, to relearn everything that you have learned in the face of your own freedom and choice, to give free rein to your dreams, visions and memories. You have the luxury of time to develop a craft, to be able to sign your work, to make or break your own destiny. Single is a time to be all that you can be by living each day as if the next time were the first time, the next love—the first love.

Those who actively feel that being single is a time of preparation refine inner resources, conceive of specific blueprints, build foundations for a home to share with a special other person, knowing all the time that when they are ready, that special person will appear, carrying resources of his or her own, ready to add to that foundation.

They know—these people who prepare with faith, trust and courage—that loneliness is only a trial of character. They intuit that there is work to be done *before* love can bloom. They sense that precious time is to be invested without grumbling *before* emotional dividends are returned. They know that they, as individuals, are *making themselves ready* for the next stage and challenge of life. They know that when they are ready from within, they will attain what they are destined to attain. They accept that being ready is up to only themselves as individuals. They trust that by being themselves and tuning their instruments, they will attract people who will recognize, appreciate, and love them because they have a center. They have something definite to give, and they know how to share it.

The trademark of these positive single people is their behavior. There is a certain relaxed quality about them. They don't push. They don't force. They don't demand love. They work, and they wait, not passively, but actively.

And then when they see the inner warmth in the smile of someone special, they don't hesitate, procrastinate or hallucinate. They see what they want, and they make a move that is serious, tender and passionate. They take time to invest in the *soul* of the special person. They love in private passion with that soulmate who was somehow "made in heaven." They resemble, in spirit, if not in body, the elephant lovers of D. H. Lawrence:

The elephant, the huge old beast,
　　is slow to mate;
he finds a female, they show no haste
　　they wait

for the sympathy in their vast shy hearts
　　slowly, slowly to rouse
as they loiter along the river-beds
　　and drink and browse

and dash in panic through the brake
　　of forest with the herd,
and sleep in massive silence, and wake
　　together, without a word.

So slowly the great hot elephant hearts
　　grow full of desire,
and the great beasts mate in secret at last,
　　hiding their fire.

Oldest they are and the wisest of beasts
　　so they know at last
how to wait for the loneliest of feasts
　　for the full repast.

They do not snatch, they do not tear;
　　their massive blood
moves as the moon-tides, near, more near
　　till they touch in flood.

The single people who see themselves preparing for a
soulmate know how to wait, how to cultivate, how to assimi-
late the idea of timing into their lives. Timing is of the essence.
The right moment must be recognized and captured, or it is
lost forever. When the time is ripe, they move. The time is
never ripe if one acts, or loves, too soon.

But others see being single as a time of completion, a permanent state of affairs, a lifelong condition in which they have a series of relationships, sensing that no one person can provide nourishment for a whole life long, and a long life at that. They have to move to stay alive. They invite new people into their lives and take nothing for granted and do not assume fate is written in the stars. They do not promise to love forever. They offer themselves in the moment, feeling that the moment is everything.

Those who see being single as a permanent condition do not expect a husband or a wife to solve all (or any) problems. In fact, they differ most noticeably from the "temporary" single in the area of expectation. Often the victim of a horrible draining divorce or a breakup they had long seen coming, this type of single person tempers all expectations and fantasies of love. They know that marriage or sustained couplings bring on a whole new set of trials, ones which can debilitate as easily as they can contaminate the freedom of the human spirit. These people often feel it should be made more difficult to get married and easier to get divorced.

Paradoxically once the *possibility* of being single turns into a *probability* for this lifetime, a pressure is taken off the shoulders of the individual. Once one accepts the inevitability of loving and sharing time with *many* different people, being single becomes a positive state, free from clutching jealousy and sterile obligations. Every experience becomes fresh with passion and possibility. Every meeting has an undercurrent of excitement. Almost anything is possible because almost nothing is expected.

Once one signs a long-term, no-cut contract with one's own singleness and individuality, the only real pressure that exists is the pressure to be *all* that one can be. Chances and risks are more readily taken. The unexpected becomes courted. The inner life becomes deeper and richer, more active and more subtle. Freedom comes out of the realm of the ideal into the realm of the real.

But both for those who see being single as a time of preparation and for those who see it as a time of completion, it is definitely a time of *self-knowledge*. Over and over again one confronts oneself with the sole responsibility for oneself. There are few excuses that can be given or accepted in front of the single mirror. The joy or the depression, the happiness or sadness, the high or the low that lives in the single's heart is largely of his or her own doing. There is nobody else to praise or blame.

No other person can ever experience the feeling in your own soul. No other person can ever do the work for you that needs to be done. No other person can supply the joy, the enthusiasm, the discipline. As a single person you have a wonderful, frightening, yet fulfilling experience *ahead* of you.

All that is past is prologue. The first-act curtain is just about to go up. The play is as adventurous, challenging and intriguing as you want it to be.

The next time is the first time.

Carry this idea with you, and it will come true.

Bon voyage!